Changing the World One Invention at a Time

Acting on Your Ideas Using the Creatively Inventing Framework

Richard Edward Rowe

iUniverse, Inc.
New York Bloomington

Changing the World One Invention at a Time
Acting on Your Ideas Using the Creatively Inventing Framework

iUniverse books may be ordered through booksellers or by contacting:

iUniverse
1663 Liberty Drive
Bloomington, IN 47403
www.iuniverse.com
1-800-Authors (1-800-288-4677)

ISBN: 978-1-4502-1983-9 (sc)
ISBN: 978-1-4502-1984-6 (ebook)
ISBN: 978-1-4502-1985-3 (dj)

Library of Congress Control Number: 2010903719

Printed in the United States of America

iUniverse rev. date: 04/9/2010

To my wonderful wife, my love, my friend, Michelle.

To my children and grandchild.

To our bunny-chasing golden retriever Maggie
and new addition Buddy.

In loving memory of Max, who continues to watch over all of us
with his big golden ears.

Finally, to the rest of my family, friends, and colleagues who share
my belief that living one's passions and following one's dreams is
what life is all about.

You know who you are.

Table of Contents

The author is not an attorney. The information contained herein is the opinion of the author and is not and should not be considered to be legal advice. Parties should seek the advice of an attorney, as appropriate, for legal and patent-related questions or issues.

No representations are made as to the accuracy of the information contained herein. The author shall not be held responsible for damage or loss of any kind due to your use of the information herein. The author does not make any warranties, express or implied (including, but not limited to, any implied warranty of merchantability and fitness for a particular purpose), relative to this book or the information contained herein.

Acknowledgments

I was lucky to have many mentors along the way, from internal company intellectual property attorneys and high-level executives to professional legal counsel who supported the companies at which I worked. I have learned from great inventor minds, physicians, philosophers, and academics. As you will learn throughout this book, I tend to ask lots of questions, and I ask those questions of people from all walks of life with different ways of looking at the world we live in. I have been fortunate to have so many great people around me who were interested in answering my questions and my e-mails.

I learned from patent attorneys Scott Weide, Terry McMillin, and Keith Moore; patent agent Dave Olynick; and attorneys Michael Abernathy, Bob Barz, and Greg Sitrick, among many others who coached and mentored me through all aspects of the patent process, from filing a patent through litigation and endless depositions as a witness. Many thanks to all of you!

I want to give a special thank you to patent attorney Pin Tan of Weide & Miller, Ltd. in Las Vegas, Nevada, who provided the reference material for Appendices A, B, C, and D. These appendices provide additional reference material covering useful information on patents and the patent process to help answer some of the common questions that inventors have asked me.

I want to thank my friends Stephen Moore, Matt Ellenthal, and Jay Walker and the other inventors and creative thinkers at Walker Digital, LLC for their inspiration and insights into the evolution of technology and building patent portfolios.

Thank you to the creative engineering team at Circadence Corporation and the management team Mike Moniz, Chris Blisard, Peter-Christian Olivo, and Rob Shaughnessy for their support and encouragement.

I want to thank my good friends Bob Bittman, Steve Morro, and Tom Baker, who encouraged and supported the gaming system inventions that the technical team at International Game Technology developed on new system technology such as Ticket-In, Ticket-Out, which helped play a role in transforming the casino industry—even when they received my e-mails at 4:00 AM.

I am also very thankful to have been inspired by so many talented inventors, creative thinkers, and innovators. I want to thank all of you but unfortunately only have room to list a few here: Jean-Louis Fiorucci, Randy Hedrick, Binh Nguyen, Craig Paulsen, Tyler Parham, Joe Kaminkow, John Acres, Bob Petrello, Tim Richards, Professor Deborah M. Gordon, and Dr. Salvatore Guarnera.

I want to especially thank Scott Weide from Weide & Miller, who took the time to read early versions of this book and provided valuable comments that helped me refine the material. Additionally, he has helped me as my patent attorney on many of the patent and patent application examples included throughout this book.

And most of all, I want to thank my wife Michelle, who continues to encourage me, even when I can be one crazy inventor building strange contraptions around the house and in the backyard!

Prologue

The first patent I ever received was while I was in the U.S. Air Force in my early twenties in the late 1970s. I don't recall who specifically pointed me in the direction of filing a patent application, but the patent itself came from a suggestion I made to save the USAF money in testing the F4E avionics systems at Homestead Air Force Base in Florida. My job required me to keep the squadron of F4Es operational. So I came up with an idea, which resulted in a patent, for a device to test the F4E test system locally, at the air force base, rather than sending it to be repaired across the country.

I went on to enjoy a career of over thirty years working at a number of corporations, leading development teams and creating products and innovations covering a wide range of technologies from system technologies and software systems to consumer products.

In 2008, I left my position as senior vice president of the intellectual property management department at a Fortune 500 company, where I was the leader of the department. I started getting requests to consult with companies on product innovation, strategy, and intellectual property development. The requests were not from a legal perspective since I am not an attorney, but rather from a practical engineering and innovation perspective.

I also helped engineers and product teams integrate product development with the development of ideas, innovations, and patent applications.

After successfully supporting requests on these topics, I decided to share the lessons I learned throughout my career with a wider audience by writing a fun and informative book on these topics.

As I researched the need for this book, I found many interesting books on the individual topics of innovation, intellectual property, strategy, and new product development. But I didn't find any books that integrated innovation with patent development from a practical or creative perspective. So I thought perhaps a book with a fresh perspective from my experience, incorporating a large number of easy-to-understand examples, might be valuable for everyone, from a person with an idea to entrepreneurs, businesspeople, engineers, and companies trying to develop new ideas, innovations, products, and markets.

As such, this book will present the information you need to transform your ideas into patent applications. The patent application provides the format to thoroughly describe your idea while also establishing your role in conceiving it. I will also show you how to evolve your existing ideas, develop new ideas, and transform those ideas into patent applications.

I struggled with the examples to use for this book, as many of my patents relate to complex technology and are generally very technical. Thus I worked to inspire your creative side and motivate you to innovate and invent while I simultaneously explain the patent process. I demonstrate the process by using fun examples without adding the additional burden of requiring you to understand the underlying technology detail. Hopefully you will enjoy these lighthearted, fun examples.

Many of the examples I used came from a patent portfolio developed as part of a company I started named Think Tek, Inc.–Think Globally based in Las Vegas, Nevada, which includes all sorts of inventions. For those readers wanting more detail associated with how a patent application is formatted and written, I have included sections from a couple of the patent applications that were filed related to the included examples.

Being a college-educated engineer with a wonderful career of practical experience, I found my engineering logic oftentimes clashed with my creative childlike self, who interrupted my logical thinking as deadlines loomed over my head with simple questions, such as "Why is that the only way to solve the problem?" "Is there a better solution for the product?" "How can we solve this problem creatively?"

Those simple questions, along with new ideas and better ways to solve the problem at hand, often clashed with the project deadline and need to get something out the door. So I needed a process where I could transform the solutions I developed from the questions I asked into inventions and document them for future products.

I found the patent process was a great way to focus my creative energy and, in some cases, the patent process enabled me to document my ideas until the marketplace caught up. I have actually heard management executives say, "Ah ha, that is exactly what the market needs." Of course, this was three or four years after I had filed a patent application on the idea. So this book will help reinforce why you should always trust your gut and act on the ideas you have. Others may just not "get it" ... yet.

I evolved this approach based on my experience into an easy-to-use process that I call the Creatively Inventing Framework. The Creatively Inventing Framework is intended to assist individual inventors and teams in transforming ideas into patent applications; it demonstrates how to solve problems, organize ideas, and integrate creative ideas into products using easy-to-follow instructional steps in a natural problem-solving methodology.

The Creatively Inventing Framework includes three stand-alone parts, described in specific chapters. Each of these parts may be used alone or may be combined as desired. For example, individual inventors may wish to use Part I and Part II of the framework, while development teams may wish to use only Part III of the framework. Regardless, the intent of each part is to simply provide a guide through specific aspects of the patent process as presented.

Along the way, you will read about the patent professionals who will ultimately help you write the patent application that will be filed with the United States Patent and Trademark Office (USPTO) and who will manage the interaction with the USPTO[1] related to your patent application.

1 USPTO Web site: uspto.gov/.

There is also a chapter with a team emphasis for inventor teams, team leaders, executives, and management staff who are searching for a repeatable innovation methodology and strategy for their businesses that can be used to establish a competitive edge. Individual inventors may also find the concepts in this chapter helpful as well.

Do all of your ideas and innovations need to be patented? Not at all; in fact, you may decide not to file patent applications on some of your ideas for any number of reasons. But should you decide to file for patent protection, this book will provide information you need to know.

Now, as we begin our creative journey through the patent process, remember, all it takes is one great idea to change the world. Perhaps it is your idea?

Chapter 1: In the Beginning, There Were Questions, Lots of Questions

For most of us, it is a struggle to take the time to think long enough about a problem or situation to solve it creatively. We tend to look for quick solutions and then move on to the next problem as we manage our lives in our on-the-go world of fast food, twenty-four-hours-a-day news channels, endless e-mails, and one meeting after another.

When we do actually find the time to think about our ideas, why does the creative process present such a challenge for so many of us? Does one either have the creative gift or not? Why are creative solutions so valuable in today's challenging business environment? I asked myself these questions to confirm the need for a whole book dedicated to the creative process of innovation and inventing, which could be valuable to private inventors, businesses, and engineers. I also asked myself some additional questions:

- Why isn't the creative process fun to most people?
- Is there a benefit in thinking about numerous solutions to a single problem and selecting the best solution? Or is solving the problem quickly a better approach?
- How can a person or a company get better at the process?

Our Fast-Paced Lives

It turns out the first thing I did in *thinking* about writing this book was to ask a bunch of questions. I even contemplated the notion of asking questions. Perhaps asking questions is something most people don't do often enough.

I remember the great questions my daughters asked while they were growing up (usually at the most inopportune time). I remember the time my daughter asked me on a busy morning, right as I was dropping her off at elementary school, "Dad, why is the sky blue?"[2] Another favorite question she asked on another day right before school was, "Dad, where does meat come from?"

Of course, I answered the questions with a quick explanation and a commitment to follow up later with more detailed explanations, and then I rushed off to work. Now, many years later, I wonder why she asked those questions at those moments and what she was thinking about at the time. Was she contemplating the meaning of those things we take for granted in our everyday lives, or was it a quick question related to something that had come up in her classroom the day before? Well, since I really didn't take the time to ask those deeper questions in the moment, I will never know. If only I would have asked her more questions. Why didn't I?

In our busy lives and in our busy business environments, taking the time to ask questions and think about answers seems to be a very low priority. Rather, rushing to get the next product into the marketplace, rushing to find a solution to a problem so the team can move to the next top issue, or rushing to drop my daughter off at school so many years ago is how most of us live our busy lives.

What if we slowed down a bit? What if we took some time to ask more questions and explore them deeper? What if we played around in our mind with possible answers to those questions, extrapolated those answers, and empowered our creative self? Where would such answers take us? Now, wouldn't these be questions worth answering?

If we could come up with answers in terms of innovations that helped enrich our daily lives or come up with innovations that might

---

2 For more information on why the sky is blue, visit the Web link: science.howstuffworks.com/sky.htm.

help the bottom line of the businesses we work at, it might turn out to be a very good experience.

Look around you. We all deal with challenges at home every day. How do we pay for groceries that keep increasing in price? How do we fill up our cars with gasoline that keeps going up and down in price? How do we deal with difficult family situations? How do we save money? How do we go on a vacation on a limited budget with limited time to do so?

We all deal with challenges in the workplace every day too. We work hard trying to fix a nagging problem with a product, trying to respond to a product by one of our competitors, trying to get a team to work together and communicate, while trying to figure out what new products consumers want to buy. Challenges confront us every day, and more often than not, we solve those challenges without really *thinking* and just move on to solve the next challenge. Perhaps we just don't have time to *think* deeper about our ideas.

Why not organize our lives and allocate time to think deeper about the questions we ask and deeper still about the answers to those questions? What if taking the time to think deeper about our solutions caused us to act on our ideas and solve our problems better, and perhaps even save us time? Now, wouldn't that be worth the *time*?

Let's start by addressing the first problem identified: taking time to think deeper about the ideas we have. Once we are able to solve our time problem, we can then explore how to act on our ideas and turn them into inventions.

Organizing Your Time

There have been many books written on time management, so let's keep things simple. Why not simply organize your schedule on a personal level and professional level and specifically allocate some time to enable you to think deeper about your ideas and the solutions to those problems nagging you? After all, allocating time for this process could ultimately lead to some rewarding discoveries. By taking the time to ask more questions and by thinking deeper about possible answers, you may be able to solve problems with better solutions and in turn make your personal life more enjoyable and your business life more successful.

Now, let's define the first step on our journey as organizing your time. I don't mean you need to schedule every minute of your day or that projects need to be organized into a long, detailed, hourly timetable. I simply mean you need to organize how you spend your time.

Spend some time thinking about what you do during the day. Are you using your time most effectively? If you are working with a team, can you organize your team to solve smaller parts of the problem, with periodic checkpoints to verify progress and raise questions?

What about your personal time: Are you using all your available time in the most efficient manner? Are you watching TV when you could be focused on the situations most important in your life?

I recently watched a video presentation on the TED Web site (www.TED.com). The presenter was Deborah M. Gordon,[3] a professor at Stanford University, and the topic was ants, which Professor Gordon studies to understand how organizations work and interact. The presentation was fascinating, as Professor Gordon described the efforts of ants and their roles within an ant colony.

An interesting aspect of her talk that caught my attention related to task allocation. Within an ant colony, a number of key tasks are performed by groups of ants when they are needed. However, approximately 50 percent of the ants within the colony that have not been allocated to a particular task *do nothing at all*. So I wondered what these ants do when they are *doing nothing*. Are they waiting to be needed? Are they providing a useful function? Professor Gordon said that these ants were "just hanging around, not doing some smaller task."[4]

Could this be analogous to how we are in the workplace or at home when we are not moving at 100 MPH or not working on a particular mission to complete a task? Don't we just hang around and let our brain go idle and coast for a while?

Sure, everyone needs time to unwind and enjoy life or, like the 50 percent of the ants in the colony described above, *just hang around*, but

3 Deborah Gordon Digs Ants. Web site: www.ted.com/talks/lang/eng/deborah_gordon_digs_ants.html; The Gordon Lab: www.stanford.edu/~dmgordon/.

4 *Ant Encounters: Interaction Networks and Colony Behavior*. Princeton Univ. Press, 2010. Link on Amazon: www.amazon.com/Ant-Encounters-Interaction-Networks-Behavior/dp/0691138796/ref=sr_1_2?ie=UTF8&s=books&qid=1262717276&sr=1-2.

how can we use time more efficiently to allocate time for exploring our ideas further?

Let's start by tracking our time by simply writing down the activities we do during a normal day at home or at work. At the end of the day, write down what you do between those activities.

Most people will find they have much more time than they think they do, which could be utilized for deeper problem solving, acting on ideas, or simply asking more questions about activities in their life.

Asking the Right Question

The next step is to start asking questions. When you are in the moment, attempting to answer a question, take a breath and make sure you are asking the *right* question. Oftentimes, we rush to find a solution and then later realize we have not asked the right question.

Give yourself time to think about the problem and understand why there is a problem. Then start asking questions about the problem. Challenge yourself to validate those questions you are asking. What questions are most appropriate given the scenario or problem?

Take the time to ask the question that is most appropriate for your problem. The following examples demonstrate how asking the right questions can lead to innovative solutions by acting on your ideas.

Basketball Example: Acting on Your Ideas

Let's say you were practicing basketball with your son, and you noticed that every time he shot the ball, it flew straight into the rim, missing the basket. You kept telling your son that if he aimed the ball higher than the rim, it would create an arc and fall into the hoop. But your son didn't really understand you and just continued repeating the scenario over and over. Then one day, you asked the general question: What can I build to get my son to arc the basketball?

You start *thinking deeper* about a variety of different devices and contraptions. You then begin asking more detailed questions: How can I get my son to aim higher than the hoop? How can I get him to throw the ball higher? Where should I have him aim when he shoots the ball?

How should he stand? Are his arms strong enough? Does he have the coordination? Am I being clear to him regarding my instructions?

Each of these questions is important, but in order to solve your problem with a specific solution, it is important to select the question you believe is the one that most accurately describes the problem. You decide the question that most accurately describes the problem is "How can I get my son to aim higher than the hoop?"

You start to think about that question and write down as many answers as you can. You could use a ten-foot stepladder placed in front of your son and tell him to shoot the basketball over it. But you decide the stepladder may partially block his view of the basketball hoop.

You come up with an idea that seems feasible and create a sketch of your solution. You build a prototype of the idea comprising a wooden frame of two-by-four boards with a large opening through which to view the basketball hoop and place the device on rollers. You position it in front of your son. The device provides him with a clear view of the basketball hoop through a large opening in the custom frame.

Now, you ask your son to throw the basketball over the frame while aiming at the basketball hoop. Your device forces your son to throw the basketball higher than the hoop and thus create an arc. In doing so, your son throws the basketball over the frame while aiming at the hoop through the large opening in the middle of the frame, and he starts making baskets. Your prototype works! You did it!

As it turns out, at least two inventors thought of similar ideas. I have included two examples, a patent application and an issued patent, on inventions similar to that described above.

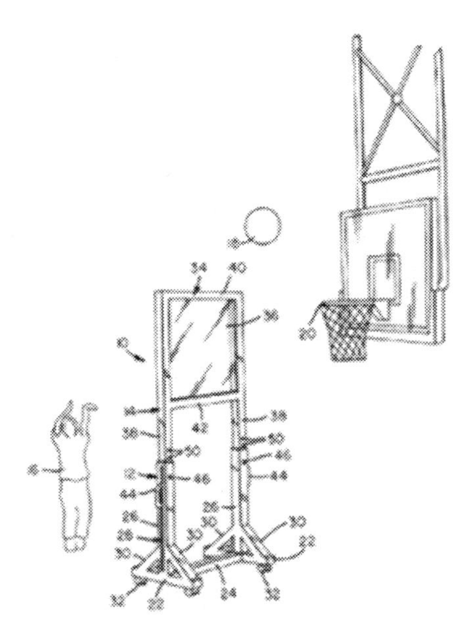

U.S. Patent Application. Inventor: Kenneth A. Hodges;
Filed 2003-02-12; Publication Number: US 2004/0157685 A1

The Patent 5,642,879 below, issued in 1997, is prior art to the patent application above, which was filed in 2003. We will discuss prior art and its implications later in the book.

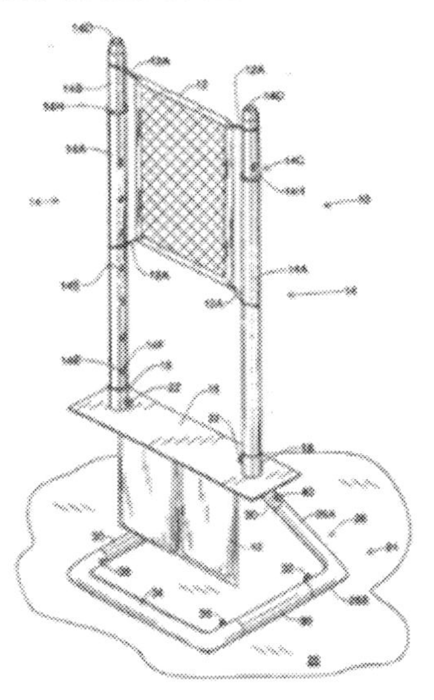

US 5,642,879 1997 Rodriguez

Example: Reflective Disposable Tissue Container

Here's another example demonstrating how asking the right questions can lead to innovative solutions. Imagine you are flying in an airplane on business. You may even have a colleague or business prospect in the seat next to you. Then, at the most unfortunate time, you sneeze. Hachoo! Well, you quickly cover your nose and mouth with your hand, possibly disgusting the person seated next to you. You might even reach for that small package of disposable tissue you carry with you when traveling.

Now, that sounds like what you would do, right? Sure, you would cover your mouth and nose with a tissue and then discretely dispose of it as quickly as possible so as not to expose your travel companion or those around you to germs.

What about those embarrassing questions that we all want to ask? "Does my nose look okay? Is it clean?" Well, I doubt you will be asking your business associate sitting next to you to please check if there is anything unseemly remaining on your nose. So what is the question you should ask about this problem?

Before you say, "Why should I bother, since I could just get up and walk to the bathroom?" think about being in a middle or window seat or during take-off or landing, when you are unable to get out of your seat.

How about, "What can I use that is easy to access and disposable and lightweight to check that my nose is not unseemly right after I sneezed when I don't want to get out of my seat?"

Notice that the question is as specific as possible, with built-in parameters that are important to the question. Let's break the question down into those parameters. Whatever I use must be the following:

- Disposable
- Lightweight
- Easy to access
- Small

Now, start to solve the problem. I would need a mirror to view my nose. But most guys don't have a mirror now, do they? Besides, mirrors are not all that lightweight or easy to access either, for most men. It might be interesting to have a mirror on your cell phone, but you would still need to locate a tissue for your nose if there was a problem.

What if the disposable package of tissue had a mirror on it? Now, that would be great, but then it wouldn't be disposable and would probably be bulky and may even be dangerous if the mirror was made of glass.

So thinking about this more, you come up with another question. "Is there a material with reflective properties that is inexpensive and could be attached to the package?"

Researching materials, you find a number of materials that are reflective but not inexpensive. You even experiment with aluminum foil but determine it does not provide enough detail of your reflection, and it wrinkles very easily, making the reflection worse.

You try other materials, but no luck. Then one weekend, you are outside in a park on a sunny afternoon and you see a child walking on the grass holding a Mylar®[5] balloon. Hey, you notice the reflection of the boy on the silver Mylar balloon material. Ah ha!

You go home and research further and after taking the time to think about possible materials, you finally find a relatively inexpensive, highly reflective Mylar material you can purchase.

There are other similar materials that will work too, but for now we stick with the Mylar material that can be cut to fit on the tissue package and affixed to the disposable tissue package permanently or temporarily in a novel way. Now that answers your initial question and provides the perfect solution!

Next, validate the parameters you previously identified by summarizing the solutions identified:

- Disposable => Reflective Mylar
- Lightweight => Reflective Mylar is lightweight
- Easy to access => Affix to disposable tissue package
- Small => Affix to disposable tissue package

5 Mylar® is a registered trademark of DuPont Teijin Films.

Have the questions been answered and has a solution been identified? Below is an image of the patent application I filed on it, which we will analyze and explore in more detail later in the book.

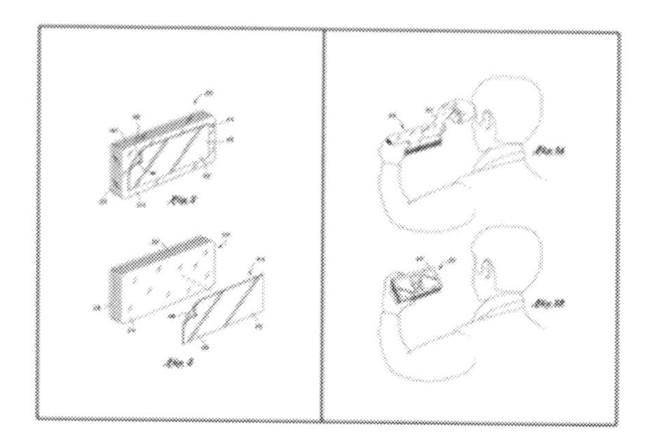

Answering Questions

And now you know the next step: answering those questions you asked. What is the most important concept to remember? Make sure you are asking the *right question* before you try to answer or provide a solution. Be prepared to ask many questions before you decide on the most appropriate question you want to answer. Then once you have that question, make sure you have enough specifics in your question to focus in on solving the problem.

Make your question as specific as possible and then come up with answers. Write down as many answers to the question as you (or your team) can come up with. Think and talk about each one, break the question down into key parameters, and try to provide a solution to each of the parameters. Finally, work out the details to match the right answers to that specific question.

Refinement

When you are trying to define the next super-popular product or a solution to a nagging problem, this process of asking questions and coming up with answers can help establish a one- or two-sentence statement that represents the specific problem that is to be solved. This is referred to as the problem statement. For our previous example, the problem statement could be "I need to check my nose after sneezing when I am traveling."

One of the most important things to remember about inventing is that you must have well-defined questions, or better yet, these well-defined questions can be framed as specific problems to be solved.

There should be many questions asked during this process, which will need to be refined into the primary questions that are most important and best frame the issue at hand where you or your team will spend time working on solutions.

Problem Statement

Formalizing the concept of asking and answering questions into the formation of a problem statement or problem definition is an even more efficient method. In fact, isn't a well-crafted question essentially a problem statement? Systematically asking many related questions that can be broken down into question parameters can quickly evolve into a well-crafted problem statement.

Example: Pet Toys

For the next example, let's explore how a team of inventors might go about the creative process. Let's say you are in charge of developing new products for a toy company. You put together a list of key questions to answer that could apply to any new product or could be tailored specifically to the toy product market.

- What do customers like about the current products?
- What do customers dislike about the current products?
- What needs have customers raised that can be provided by enhancing or modifying current products?
- What needs have customers raised that can be translated into a product?
- What are ideas for new products?
- What are ideas for product features?
- What are the most popular products being sold today?

- What market has shown growth in the last two years?
- What are people spending on products in these markets?

Your team does the research and, interestingly enough, they find that the market for pet toys is a fast-growing one. Your team realizes that people are continuing to spend money on their pets; pet toys are now on your team's radar. Your team asks more questions.

- Which pets are most popular?
- Who spends more, cat owners or dog owners?
- How many people own cats versus how many people own dogs?
- What are the biggest challenges for pet owners?

Your team works on the answers to the questions and fills in the blanks with educated assumptions based on their research while also adding more questions. The team finds a great resource of information to help answer their questions from the American Pet Products Manufacturers Association (APPMA). It is a summary of industry statistics and trends: www.appma.org/press_industrytrends.asp.

How many households in the United States own a pet?

Answer: According to the APPMA survey in 2007–2008, 63 percent of U.S. households own a pet, equating to 71.1 million homes.

How much is spent on pets in the United States?

Answer: According to the APPMA survey in 2007–2008, $43.4 billion is projected for 2008.

How many people own cats versus how many people own dogs?

Answer: According to the APPMA survey in 2007–2008, 38.4 million households own cats while 44.8 million households own a dog.

How much do cat owners spend on toys on average per year versus dog owners?

Answer: According to the APPMA survey in 2007–2008, cat owners spend on average $26 per year on toys while dog owners spend $41 per year on toys. The team does some simple calculations using the information and determines that U.S. pet cat owners spend $998.4 million on cat toys per year while U.S. pet dog owners spend $1.8 billion on dog toys per year.

The team realizes that the products for dogs will be different from the products for cats. As such, the team decides to focus on dog toys and dog exercise equipment. The team further notes that this decision was not driven by a specific business opportunity. Rather, the team consists of primarily dog lovers and decided to focus on dog products based on the passion for dogs shared within the team.

What are the biggest challenges for dog owners?

Answer: Using a variety of different sources, the team comes to the conclusion that time to exercise their dogs due to the consumer's busy schedule is the biggest problem for most U.S. households that own a dog. This becomes even more of a challenge for those dog owners who live in busy city centers with limited space for active dogs.

The team develops a problem statement for their project:

Dog owners with busy work schedules and limited space have a problem exercising their dogs.

Your team is now focused on a pet dog toy that could be used to exercise their dog without requiring the dog owner to exert a large amount of energy or use a large amount of space. You realize a product addressing this problem could be a very popular product among dog owners.

Example: The Remote-Controlled Dog Toy

The team researches popular dog toys on the market today and comes up with a large number of new product ideas. The team evaluates the ideas and reviews the problem statement.

Some ideas are put on the back burner as other ideas are reviewed. Finally, one of the team members throws out a new idea: What if we create a remote-controlled car and attach a small stuffed animal to the car's frame? Now that would be fun for both the dog and the owner! It would exercise the dog and could be operated in a small space.

Yes! The team agrees to focus on this new remote-controlled dog toy. More questions are asked, which leads to the need for prototypes to test their new remote-controlled dog toy idea and answer their questions:

- Are stuffed animals safe for dogs to chew and put in their mouths?
- How could the stuffed animal be affixed to the remote-controlled car?
- Will dogs chase it?
- How will the dog react when the dog catches the toy?

The team builds a prototype by taking a car frame off a remote-controlled car and uses heavy tape to secure a stuffed animal to the frame. To test the prototype, team members use the prototype with their own dogs and report the results back to the team. The findings are interesting:

- If the toy is too large, the dog just barks at the device or takes cover and gets out of the way as the owner controls it around the house. If the toy is similar to the size of a small rabbit or squirrel, the dog chases it. But that depends on the dog, as some little dogs will chase large toys but some large dogs won't chase the same large toys.
- When the dog catches it, it chews the stuffed animal.
- The dog may also want to pick the toy up when it catches it, but may not be able to do so when the toy is attached to the frame of the remote-controlled car.

- One team member notices when they put a large stuffed animal on the frame, their three-year-old child loves to chase the toy around the house more than the dog does. (Although not the invention, the dog is entertained by watching the three-year-old and runs around the house, chasing the three-year-old.)

The team comes up with questions and answers around each of the observations:

1. What size toy is optimal for the dog's size?
2. Are there stuffed animals available that are approved by the American Kennel Club (AKC) that dogs use today?
3. How can the toy be engineered to release the stuffed animal when the dog catches it?
4. How can the toy be adapted to work for dogs or small children?

- Questions 1 and 2: The team finds that their local pet store has bins full of different sized stuffed animals for dogs and finds out from the store manager that the stuffed animals are very popular and approved by the AKC. Perfect!
- Question 3 is a bit more complicated and will require a number of prototypes to test. After a series of trials and errors, they use a small piece of Velcro®[6] that seems to do the trick. It's inexpensive and easily attached to the stuffed animal and the remote-controlled car frame. The team also contemplates if such a release capability would defeat the purpose of minimizing the amount of interaction required by the owner due to the need to reattach the stuffed animal each time the dog catches it. After some debate, it is decided that the release capability approach is preferred to focus the dog on chewing the stuffed animal versus the dog chewing on the hard plastic remote-controlled car.
- Question 4 is even more complicated and requires the entire team to work together to come up with possible answers.

6 Velcro® is a registered trademark of Velcro Industries B. V.

One of the team members comes up with the idea of an adjustable frame in the shape of a square that can expand from a small square to a large square, providing a base for small stuffed toys or large stuffed toys, providing the consumer with the flexibility to place the optimal size stuffed toy for their dog on the toy. The frame is attached to the base of a remote-controlled car, and Velcro is used on the frame to attach the toy.

The team tests out this new prototype and determines that the remote-controlled toy works well for his or her dogs (in addition to their young children) by placing various sized stuffed animals onto the frame. This provides a toy for a dog and can be changed to a larger stuffed animal to provide a toy for a young child.

Now, let's go back and review the problem statement:

Dog owners with busy work schedules and limited space have a problem exercising their dogs.

Has a product been developed that addresses this problem?

Yes. In fact, the team developed three patent applications covering this technology.

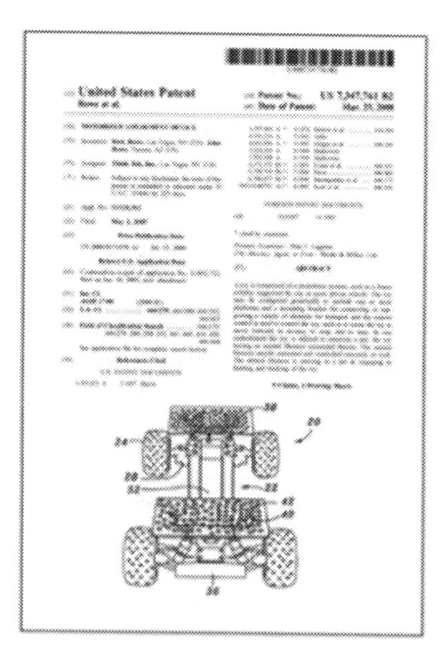
United States Patent

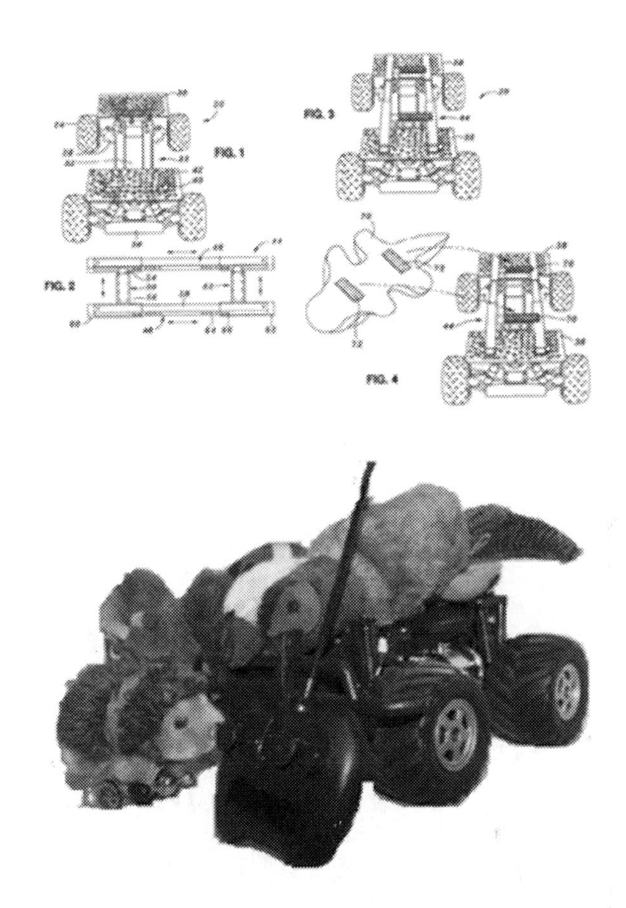

Part I: Four-Step Opportunity Spotlight

Let's summarize the process presented in this chapter into Part I of the Creatively Inventing Framework: the "Four-Step Opportunity Spotlight." It highlights the specific problem to be solved and where you will focus.

1. Asking the right questions
2. Answering questions
3. Refinement
4. Problem statement

Chapter 2: Creative Prototypes and Experimentation

A chapter on creative prototypes and experimentation must begin with one of my favorite quotes. After working endlessly on perfecting the light bulb, Thomas Edison was reported to have said, "I have not failed 1,000 times. I have successfully discovered 1,000 ways not to make the light bulb." Ultimately, we are fortunate he stuck with it.[7]

Innovation oftentimes requires experimentation once a problem statement or idea is defined. In some cases, experimentation could simply take the form of theoretical implementation, also known as constructive reduction to practice, without having to develop anything physically. An example of constructive reduction to practice is the

7 You can use the link www.archives.gov/ to search for an image of the U.S. patent Edison received on the light bulb at the National Archives and Records Administration.

patent application that will be described in detail in later chapters. Other situations may require experimentation and the development of prototypes to get real-world feedback on an attempted solution.

We've explored how an individual and a team might ask questions, come up with answers, and identify opportunities by defining a problem statement and asking more questions. The process can be very logical and process oriented, progressively working toward a product that answers the questions and solves the problem. But how do you get yourself (or your team) into a creative and innovative mind-set?

There was a popular IBM commercial where a boss walks into a dark room and finds his entire team laying on the floor with their eyes closed. He turns the light on and asks the group, "What are you doing in here?" The team responds, "Innovating." The stunned boss turns the light off and leaves the room.

Is that what it takes to innovate? Do you need to meditate in a quiet place? Is brainstorming the way to innovate? Is problem solving the way to innovate? Is waiting for that cool idea innovating? Let's face it, there are many experts out there who will share their ideas on how to innovate, but more often than not, the methodologies presented are only as successful as those who believe in them. In other words, there are many different techniques to get into the mind-set for innovating and getting excited about pushing the envelope and taking risks.

But what mind-set are we really talking about? What does being creative really mean? What does innovation really mean? Why is innovation sometimes considered risk taking? Well, here I go again, asking questions to try and understand the problem I want to solve.

So let's discuss these topics, not from a psychological or academic perspective, but from the perspective of a person tasked with the challenge of providing innovation, or more specifically, the person on the hook to develop products that customers want to purchase. Let's discuss this from the perspective of a curious person who loves technology and loves to experiment, prototype, and solve problems. In other words, let's discuss this from my perspective.

Creatively Developing Ideas

I like to think of being creative as looking at the world without limitations, throwing away the walls and the rules that we all tend to take for granted. No doubt at some point, reality does have to be integrated into the process. But before the cold water splashes you in the face, have some fun with the notion of creating your own reality and extrapolate. Experiment with your ideas and try to build them. Keep a journal of your results. This is called prototyping, and as you will see, it is an important part of creatively inventing.

The way I like to start is to first clear my head and think about a topic. I start by asking "what if" questions and see where they lead me. Let's try an off-the-cuff example and see where this goes.

Example: The Zucchini Trellis

First, we need to pick a topic. Let's choose a fun, green-tech topic: growing zucchini in a confined area in the desert. Prior to embarking on developing a solution, the process of research, as demonstrated with the dog toy invention, is important. As such, we could get on the Internet and Google the topic and look for information on the topic. We could go to the bookstore and buy books on making a garden and learning what we need. But what if we did not do this research before trying to solve the problem? What if we just jumped right in and started experimenting with prototypes? What sort of solution would we come up with?

Understanding the Problem to Solve

What I know about zucchini is that it needs plenty of sun and plenty of water and good rich soil to grow in. I know from seeing zucchini plants in the past that the zucchini grows on a vine and requires a tremendous amount of space. Let's break this down into some key components:

1. Need seeds
2. Need a space to grow our plant
3. Need plenty of water

4. Need rich soil
5. Need plenty of sun

Now, I ask myself, are these the key elements I need to grow zucchini? I conclude that yes, these five items are the key elements I need to address to grow zucchini. Next, I go through the list and see if I need to innovate or if there is a simple solution.

1. Need seeds. Okay, this an easy one. I can buy those from the grocery store.
2. Need a space to grow our plant. I think of my backyard and realize this one is probably a bit more challenging. So let's come back to it.
3. Need plenty of water. Thanks to my local water supply company in the city I live in, no problem here. However, I will need to use some sort of distribution system to water the plants most effectively. That is, I might need to use a drip system or a regular sprinkler. So let's come back to this element as well.
4. Need rich soil. Easily solved with a bag of soil and fertilizer from the local nursery.
5. Need plenty of sun. Okay, this one is an easy one too, since I live in the desert.

Did I think of any other key elements or requirements as I reviewed my list? Perhaps I might want to determine if there are different types of zucchini for growing in a low humidity climate. Or there may be certain types of zucchini that are more tender or tasty than others. But I determine that instead of buying the seeds from the grocery store, I will buy the seeds at the nursery when I pick up the soil and fertilizer I need. So my plan has expanded a bit with some action items. Let's summarize where we are now:

1. Need seeds. Easily solved, pick up at grocery store or nursery.
2. Need a space to grow our plant. Action item: need to identify a space where the plant can grow in my backyard.

3. Need plenty of water. Thinking about this more, I determine a drip system is all I really need. So all I need to do is identify a location where I can tap into my existing drip system in the backyard.
4. Need rich soil. Action item: pick up some soil and fertilizer at the local nursery.
5. Need plenty of sun. Easily solved, since I live in the desert.

This leaves us with really only one item to think about, and that would be item number 2. With some basic understanding of what we are trying to accomplish and the questions remaining, let's define the problem statement:

How can zucchini be grown in a confined area in a desert climate?

A Preliminary Design

Now, let's try to solve our main challenge of growing zucchini in a confined area. Most of us have limited space in our backyards, so it is definitely a challenge to find a place where the long vines of a zucchini plant can grow to get as much sun as possible. Hey, what did I just say? Yes, I said vines. Well, what if I treated the zucchini plant as a vine, sort of like a grapevine, and grew the plant on a trellis or fence? Thinking about this more, the water hits me in the face as I realize that I would need to support the heavy zucchinis that will ultimate grow on the vine.

What if I were to create a trellis that had some additional space in front of it and behind it to build a support system for those zucchinis that grow? Hmm, I start to visualize a wire trellis built in a way to support the plant while also providing space for the zucchinis to be supported.

The trellis is pretty easy. I can use chicken wire and create a three-foot-high circular structure by taking a piece of chicken wire and shaping it into a two-foot-diameter circle and use wooden dowels about four feet long as support stakes that can be driven into the ground about one foot. Thinking about this more, I realize I will need to drill about four or five 1/8-inch holes in the dowel and then use some regular wire to attach the dowel to the circular piece of chicken wire.

Of course, I need to identify a location in the backyard that gets full sun and has drip system access. I will dig up the existing desert soil in a circle a little larger than my chicken wire frame in which to place the rich soil I will purchase from the nursery. Now, all I need to do is figure out how to support the heavy zucchini plants I will be growing on this circular chicken wire trellis.

I think about this for a little while and try to visualize how the vines look as they grow all around the trellis. I can visualize the flowers that bloom and turn into zucchinis. They could be located anywhere on the trellis. Hmm, this is a bit of a challenge. I feel the splash of cold water hitting my face and start to doubt that this solution I have dreamed up will actually work. But then I feel a wave of optimism come over me. Heck, I can solve this problem. So I start visualizing various scenarios.

I could build wooden shelves inside the chicken wire and, as the zucchini plant blooms, add shelves as needed. Or I could create a wooden structure around the outside of the circular chicken wire trellis. It could be in the shape of a square. I could then arrange pieces of plywood as shelves to provide to a support system for the zucchinis as they grow.

I realize that I need to make sure I don't block the sun, so I start to think about the circular design with the shelves on the outside of the chicken wire and wonder if I should just build a straight section of chicken wire with layers of shelves in the front and the back. I sketch out both options to see which works the best.

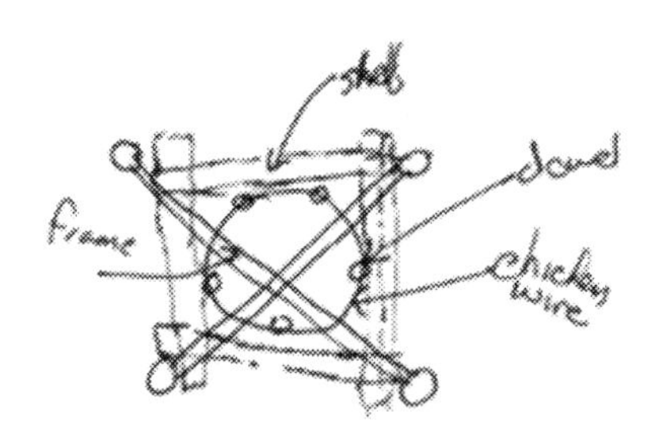

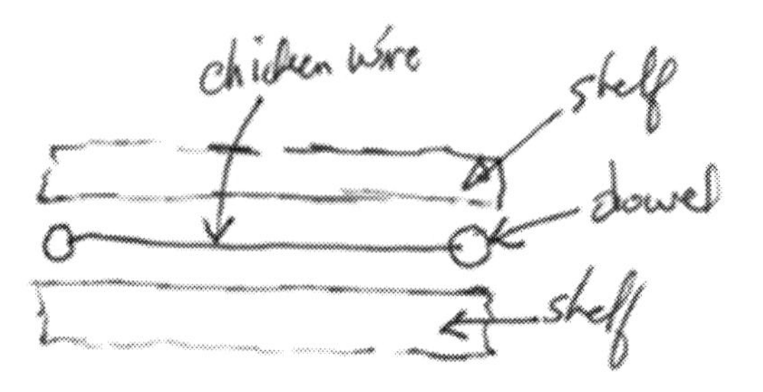

After spending a few minutes drawing out both options, I quickly realize the circular design is much more complicated than the simple straight-section design. I am impressed with my detailed design and the idea behind it to support the multiple shelves to place the zucchini as they grow. I recall a principle called "Occam's razor," which was named after a fourteenth-century logician and Franciscan friar William of Occam.

Okay, I realize thinking of Occam's razor is actually a little distracting, as we are only dealing with a simple chicken wire zucchini growing system. But Occam's razor provides a basic principle that we can use as a general rule of thumb: "When you have two competing theories that make exactly the same predictions, the simpler one is the better."[8] So we will just adapt this general principle to our project design and restate it a bit: ***When we have two competing designs that do the same thing, the simpler one is the better one.***

Great, now we have a general rule that we can follow as we further develop our design. So which design is the simpler solution? Well, that doesn't take long to decide: the straight piece of chicken wire with a single row of shelves is what we will build.

8 Gibbs, Phil. 1997 article in May 2009 compilation. "What is Occam's Razor?" in Don Koks, Usenet Physics FAQ. math.ucr.edu/home/baez/physics/General/occam.html.

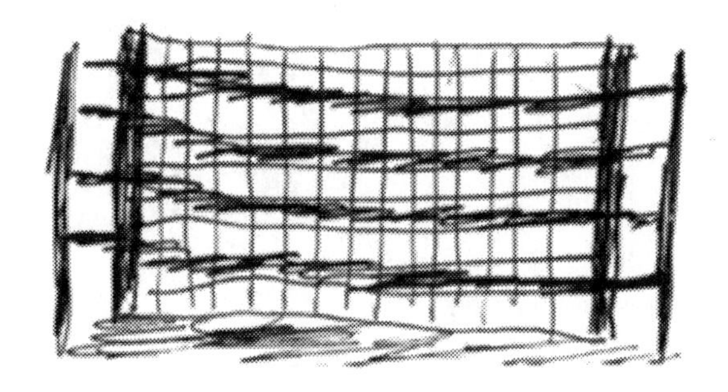

With my design ready and sketched out on paper, I go into the backyard and look for the perfect spot to dig out some holes in preparation for planting. As I am looking, I notice a rabbit feasting on my grass. A rabbit in the desert, you ask? Yes, I hadn't thought of it before, but my golden retriever loves to sit on the couch looking out the backyard window, scanning for those little creatures. Usually when she sees one, she starts barking frantically until I go into the backyard and scare it off.

The second thing I notice is that desert soil is not very good soil and is as hard as cement. Well, there goes my original plan out the window. But wait! That's just part of experimenting, inventing, and prototyping, isn't it? Sure, okay, let's solve the problem and adapt our design.

Defining Problem Statements

First, let's identify the latest challenges:

1. How do we keep rabbits from eating our zucchini?
2. How will the zucchini grow in soil that is as hard as cement? Can we dig out a hole sufficiently large enough to fill with soil purchased from the nursery to allow the zucchini to establish a nice root system for growth? How wide does it need to be? How deep does it need to be?

The first question seems to be easily solved by putting chicken wire around the area in which we grow the zucchini, or having some sort of small wall around the garden area. However, the second question is a bit more complicated. No way do I want to use the pick and shovel along with dynamite to blow a hole in the backyard. It really doesn't sound too appealing, so let's take the simple approach. How about getting a planter box or a large pot and fill it with fertile potting soil? Yes, that seems to solve both our issues above. It will keep the plants off the ground while also providing plenty of room for the zucchini to establish a root structure.

1. How do we keep rabbits from eating our zucchini?
   Use a planter box or large pot high enough to prevent a pesky rabbit from jumping into the zucchini.
2. How will the zucchini grow in soil that is as hard as cement, or probably a better question, how can we dig out a hole sufficiently large to allow the zucchini to establish a nice root system for growth?
   Use a planter box or large pot.

Now, I head over to my local nursery full of determination. I arrive, grab a cart, and go in search of the supplies I will need. I walk around and collect all my supplies:

- Potting soil and fertilizer.
- Planter box or large pot. I decide on two fifteen-gallon plant containers.
- Zucchini seeds. I ask the workers at the nursery about the seeds, and they recommend I use small, young zucchini plants, which will save me a great deal of time.
- Tubing to attach to the existing drip system.
- Wood and chicken wire. I realize that I will have to go to the hardware store for those. But I see a number of already-built wooden lattices that are the perfect size. I buy two six-foot lattices, one to place behind each of the fifteen-gallon containers.
- Wooden structure to place growing zucchinis. I decide to go to the hardware store once my vines grow.

I return from the nursery and begin to build my invention. I find the perfect spot that will get plenty of sun, put the large containers in place, fill them up with potting soil, plant the small zucchini plants in place, attach the tubing with a couple of two-gallon-an-hour drippers in each container, place the lattice behind each container, and thoroughly water both containers. I take a look at my creation and feel pretty good about myself. Now, all I need to do is wait for the plants to grow and attach the vines to the lattice.

Over a twenty-four-hour period, I check on the plants. Obviously, I am excited to have the plants grow, but I realize my checking on them will not make them grow any faster. I take a look at the plants in the container and see that all of their large leaves are in odd positions and flattened, as if someone had stepped on them. I look around the yard and it hits me—a gust of wind 40 MPH! Whoosh! Yes, another element of the desert location that I live in, besides low humidity, is wind. I get lots of wind, and sometimes it is very strong. Well, I have a new problem.

- How can I create a wind block without blocking the sun?
- How can I build it strong enough to not get blown away like a kite when the wind hits it?

I start thinking again and decide I could build a small greenhouse over the entire structure. Well, so much for my simple design! Thinking about this more, I realize a greenhouse in temperatures above 100 degrees may not be as smart as I first thought. I liked cooked zucchini, but only after it is fully grown.

What if I created a wind block that used clear plastic to let the sunrays through, without a top? Since heat rises, that would keep from increasing the temperature around the zucchini.

I will need a frame, maybe wooden, to attach the plastic. I could use the plastic wrap used to keep food fresh, but I'm not sure that is strong enough. Since this requires some additional information I don't have, I decide to head off to the hardware store and see if they have anything I could use to keep the design simple and to prevent it from becoming a kite in large wind gusts.

As I go through the design in my mind, I realize that any square structure would take the full force of the desert winds. That could be nearly 40 to 50 MPH at times where I live.

What if I create two wood frame panels and then place them together in a V shape, with the point of the V headed toward the direction where the wind comes from most often? That should be easy to build too: I just need to make two frames, attach the heavy-duty plastic wrap, form the V shape, and secure them in place with stakes and possibly a support beam across the top of the V shape.

For some reason, I keep having a vision of my V-shape structure being taken up one thousand feet in the air by a wind gust. That would not be a pleasant sight for my neighbors, but it might scare off a rabbit or two.

Back to work. I pick out a list of supplies, including wood for a frame, stakes to secure the assembled wind block, screws, wires, and heavy-duty tape. I come across a clear piece of Plexiglas that would be perfect, but the cost of it compared to the plastic wrap prevents me from buying it.

Now, let's check to ensure that I have addressed the issues I identified before I started to build the wind-blocking device:

How can I create a wind block without blocking the sun?

- Create two frames, each frame will be made out of five one-inch by four-inch by six-foot pieces of wood.
- Create a square out of four of them and then put the fifth piece of wood in the center to support the frame, securing them all in place with wood screws.
- Use layer after layer of plastic wrap across one side of the panel, attaching it with heavy-duty tape along all sides, including the middle support beam. I put a few nails into the tape to ensure everything stays secure.

How can I build it strong enough to not get blown away like a kite when the wind hits it?

- Each frame will be secured in place by stakes to form a V facing the direction of the wind.
- A small piece of wood will be placed across the top of the V to form an A, to ensure the wood sides don't collapse when the wind blows.

- Attach the bottom of the frame to a stake to secure the bottom in place.

Building a Prototype

As I have already mentioned, there is no better experience than that of lessons learned by doing. So I build both frames. Once completed, I see they are pretty large. I know, I should have realized that when I was picking out six-foot-long pieces of wood. But actually seeing a prototype of the device you are building puts everything into perspective, and oftentimes you may come to the realization that your design is a bit larger than you had originally thought.

So I decide to secure the plastic wrap to one of the frames first to see how everything works. I lay row after row of plastic wrap on the frame. Just a side note here: people driving by my house must have wondered what the heck I was doing putting plastic wrap on a six-foot wooden frame.

Once completed, I check it out, and it appears pretty darned secure. But rather than trying to complete the second frame, I decide to give it a test and take it outside into the elements to see how it holds up to the wind. Today is a typical day with 20 MPH winds. Off I go into the backyard. The wind hits the structure, and I almost lose my balance. If anyone was watching me at this moment, they would surely think I had lost it.

I negotiate the wind and head to the two containers I have outside. I reach the area, and again the rush of a cold splash of reality strikes me as I see the size of this monstrous structure. Now I remember why I made it six feet: the trellis, of course! When the zucchini plant eventually grows, there will be six feet of vines that need to be protected from the full force of the desert winds.

I take a step back and think for a minute, as I look at the two containers and the location I have placed the containers. Wait a minute, I can create a simple lean-to frame and just lay it on its side, where the top of the frame will lay on top of the trellis and the bottom of the frame will be on the ground in front of the containers. I put it into place; hmm, this works and the sides are open so the heat shouldn't build up too much under the plastic.

The wind starts to build, but I haven't secured it in place yet. Go figure; the reality of prototyping. I just figured there would be no wind when I set this up. Now, the structure starts to move around, and images of the flying kite nightmare come back into my head. I quickly pound in a couple of stakes, place a nail on either side of the structure to secure some wire, and then secure each piece of wire to the stake below.

Gust after gust now, and the darned structure is holding pretty well. I look at the zucchini below, and the young plants are only slightly moving. Hey, it is working. I notice I have a tear or two in the plastic wrap and quickly use my heavy-duty tape to patch them. It is working, and actually I am quite pleased with myself. Now, I just need to wait and see how it goes over the course of a few days.

I remember I have the other frame, so for now I decide to place it aside until I see if this design is going to work. Let's review our outstanding issues and see how the design changed.

How can I create a wind block without blocking the sun?

- Create two frames.—*Correction, I only needed one frame.*

How can I build it strong enough to not get blown away like a kite when the wind hits it?

- Each frame will be secured in place by stakes to form a V facing the direction of the wind.—*Correction, I used a single frame and placed it at an angle from the trellis to the ground in a lean-to position.*
- A small piece of wood will be placed across the top of the V to form an A to ensure the wood sides don't collapse when the wind blows.—*Correction, no need for this anymore.*
- Attach the bottom of the frame to a stake to secure the bottom in place.—*Correction, the stake was placed into the ground, but a nail was hammered into the side of the frame to attach the wire. The wire reached the stake and was secured to it.*

After a few days of checking how the structure works in the wind, it appears to have passed the test.

Experimenting with Prototypes

The plastic wrap is holding nicely. The structure itself remains securely in place attached to the stakes; the wind has not launched it on a flight around the neighborhood. With that design in place and working, we need to think of the big picture. Eventually, there will be vines secured to the trellis by small pieces of wire or gardening tape. In fact, I am visualizing vines completely covering the trellis and nice flowers in the locations where zucchinis will grow. Then my mind continues and I visualize the flowers turning into zucchinis and growing bigger and bigger, hanging from the trellis. The zucchinis get heavier and heavier and ultimately cause the trellis to break or the zucchinis to fall off. What did we forget?

Ah ha! Of course, we had envisioned the need for a structure to be placed in front of the trellis to support the growing zucchinis. My early design used a wooden frame that included a number of wooden shelves for the zucchinis to grow.

Sketching the design out, it looks good enough but as I start to think more about it and visualize how it will work, I realize that the structure itself will block the sun from the vines. That might be a problem since zucchini plants love and, more importantly, need the sun on their leaves. So how might we make the design better?

I could use string in place of wood for the shelf or maybe even a net-like arrangement to support the growing zucchinis, which would allow plenty of sunlight to reach the zucchini leaves. Thinking about this more, I realize a single piece of string doesn't seem strong enough to support the zucchinis. What if I used our one-inch by four-inch by six-foot piece of wood that was in the frame we set aside and made a frame that extended to either side of the trellis and was as tall as the trellis? Perhaps run a two-by-four around the outside to reinforce the strength and stability of the frame.

In other words, the sides of the frame would run from the ground to the same height as the top of the trellis. We could start the string shelves a few inches above the container and run them up to the top of the trellis. A zucchini can grow to about three or four inches in diameter or larger. However, we need to provide the greatest coverage possible for both young small plants and older larger plants. The nice side effect of using string is it will allow some movement without damaging the zucchini as it grows.

My mind visualizes the four or five large zucchinis growing on a single row of string. Using three strings for each row should be strong enough to support the zucchinis, but is there a better way to design this?

I could run string straight down from the top, but would need an additional piece of wood on the bottom of the frame right above the container, which could be used to attach the strings. Additionally, we could use three vertical strings and weave the vertical strings under a horizontal string and then over the next horizontal string to help keep the string in place as the zucchinis grow.

I could even play with the string mesh pattern, and instead of using horizontal and vertical strings, which create a mesh of square patterns to support the growing zucchinis, I could attach the string to the frame at an angle and create a diamond pattern to support the zucchinis instead.

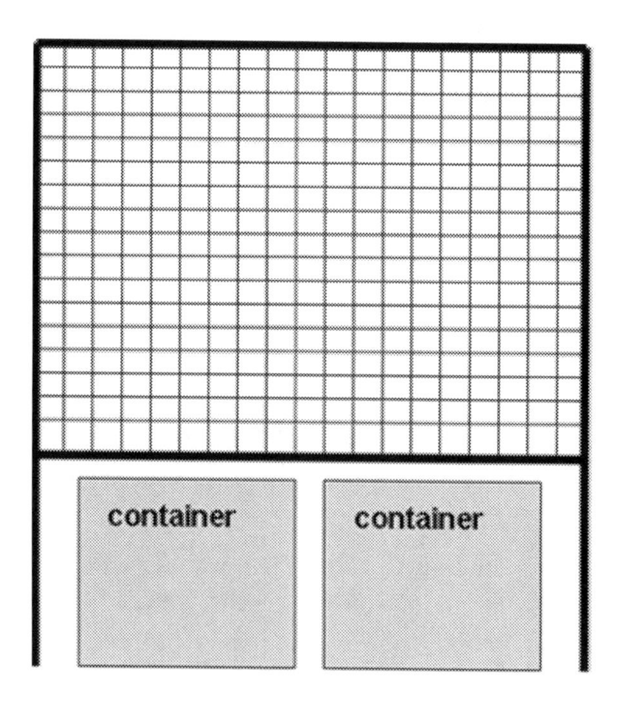

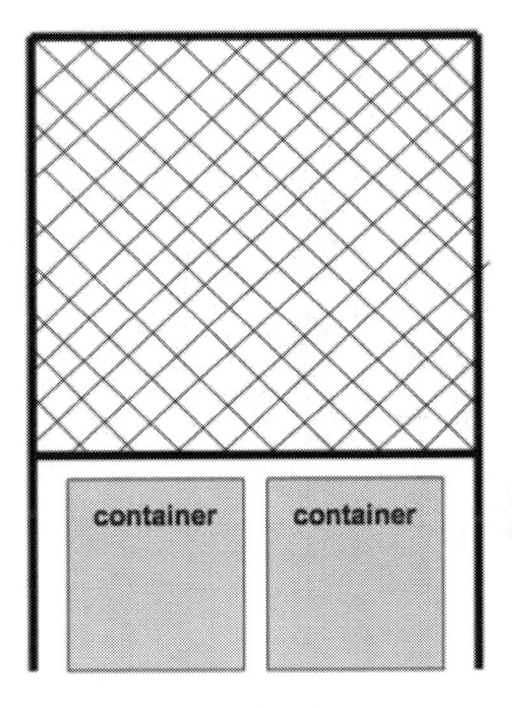

With three strings for each of the lines shown in the drawing, each of the strings would be spaced evenly apart by securing one string on the edge of one side of the frame, another string in the middle, and another string on the other edge of the one side of the frame.

Here is a cutaway section view:

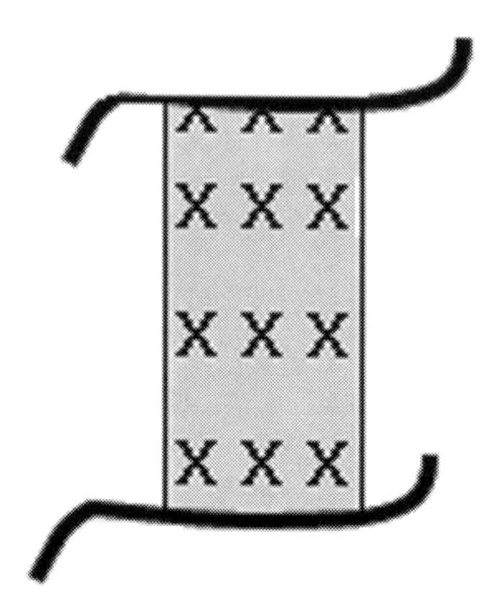

Now, as the zucchinis grow, the support extends to the width of the piece of wood used for the frame, or four inches. I intuitively like the diamond shape better as it seems to give the zucchinis more support as they grow.

The next task we need to do is place a couple of pieces of wire on the top of the frame to attach it to the top of the trellis. We need to ensure there is plenty of space to work with the growing zucchini plants to get them started on the string matrix, but not too much space. Using wire, we will be able to adjust the frame easily. Let's also place a stake on each leg of the frame so it won't move around as it gets heavy with zucchinis.

The last thing we need to do now is to adjust our lean-to design to provide space for the frame that will hold our zucchinis. Simply adding two horizontal pieces of wood to create a space between the top of the trellis and the top of the lean-to should provide the zucchini frame with plenty of space. It also provides a path for heat to escape upward instead of becoming trapped under the lean-to. Let's now give it a few weeks for the plants to grow and see how our design worked.

Three Weeks Later: Reassessing the Project

It has been roughly three weeks now and the need for additional changes to the design has become obvious. As the plants were growing, there have been numerous high-wind days. A few of the days had wind gusts between 45 MPH and 65 MPH.

Amazingly, our plastic wrap wind block has held up surprising well. A few additional pieces of plastic wrap and some additional tape were all that was needed to hold everything in place. I had to also place wood pieces on one side of the structure to block the wind from coming in from the side, which appeared to happen often. Surprisingly, the overall design held together nicely given the unplanned weather challenges.

Thinking back on the design, it would probably have been smart (albeit much more expensive) to use clear Plexiglas pieces secured to the frame. However, I did learn something extremely interesting: plastic wrap will hold up in 60 MPH winds full on.

I must say I am not sure how useful that bit of knowledge is, since most people don't use plastic wrap to block wind. I suppose if a camper needed a wind shelter, heck, a plastic wrap wind block could be useful.

Looking at how the zucchini was growing was also surprising. Another bit of information that would probably be obvious had I done some research before starting the project was that the plant really grew like a weed. So trying to train it to grow on a traditional trellis was close to impossible without breaking the vines. So the design needed to be modified yet again. We will need to innovate from our original design.

This time, let's use an eight- to twelve-inch by one-inch by six-foot piece of wood for each side and use a couple pieces of wood along the top to hold it in place to make a frame with a small piece of wood lower, around the height of the container, to stabilize the entire frame. Now, let's go back to our three horizontal string approach and forget about the vertical string supports and see how it does.

With this design, the vine should grow upward through the pieces of string, which will be in place to both help secure the vine as it grows and support the zucchinis as they grow. We will just have to diligently weave the growing vine through the strings.

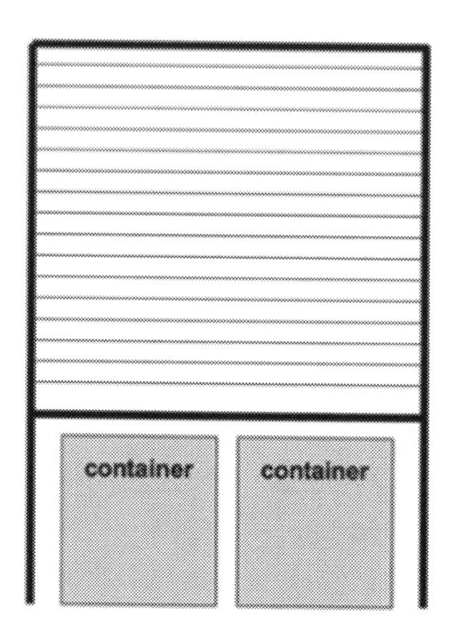

To help us focus on the growing zucchinis, we should upgrade our design to include the Plexiglas wind block to prevent the sort of problems we had early on. This will enable easy access to help manage the growth of the plant. It will also enable inspection of the zucchinis to verify one or more of the string supports are supporting them as they grow.

As illustrated in the images shown, the design worked pretty well, and the zucchini plant grew incredibly well. The one remaining major problem I encountered was related to the heat. It turned out that since the plastic containers were located above the ground, and since I chose a western-facing location that received full sun close to a block wall, which radiated an incredible amount of heat, the soil within the plastic container became very hot and prevented zucchinis from transforming from flower to zucchini.

The lesson learned here is that the plants should have been planted below the ground level in a location away from a block wall that radiated heat. As for those pesky rabbits wanting to snack on the zucchinis, a simple chicken wire barrier would easily keep them away.

Even with this setback, the lessons learned from experimenting with prototypes will be applied next season to a "planted below ground" version. Better yet, I may even be able to convince my wonderful wife to allow me to grow a scaled-down version of the plant in the temperature-controlled house. Then again, inviting bees within my house may not be the smartest idea. But on a serious note, if I did want to grow the plant indoors, I would need to manually pollinate the plant. It turns out this is not that big of a stretch, and I found numerous articles on the Internet describing how this could be done. Stay tuned …

Final Thoughts on the Zucchini Trellis Design

Taking a step back and looking at our design, I have to wonder what other sort of fruit and vegetables that grow similarly to zucchini could be grown using this design. Certainly all forms of squash and maybe even watermelon. Now that would be a sight to see! However, the frame would have to be much larger with a nicely supported matrix of string to hold the watermelon in place.

For garden lovers who live in the city (also known as urban farmers), this design might be just the invention needed to grow zucchini. Or for the farmer or city dweller with limited space for growing something like zucchini, this invention could help grow more fruits and vegetables in less space, such as a greenhouse or even outside an apartment. Implementing this example into a kit of easy-to-assemble plastic parts could further refine this somewhat crude prototype. The kit could be made in various sizes and put together by the consumer. Let's give our invention the name: *A Vertical Growing Apparatus and Method.*

Interesting how a design changes as you build a prototype and attempt to use it in the real world. Not doing basic research as needed for a project is a mistake many new inventors make. For example, I had naively thought I could grow the plant like a vine up a trellis. Well, what I discovered about zucchini was it grows similar to a weed and grows in a cluster with large leaves, thereby requiring my trellis design to be completely rebuilt and integrated with the zucchinis using rows of string that could support the leaves as they grew and the zucchinis once the grew too.

I also painfully realized that growing anything in the desert would need protection from the winds, which can go from 0 to 65 MPH faster than a Porsche. So the wind block became an important part of the design. Once that issue was addressed, the zucchini was able to grow large enough to flower.

While this example was a fun green-tech example, the same process and issues happen with all projects, from the simple low-tech projects to the highly technical and complex projects. So while this project cost me less than $200 to construct, the project could have been a new multimillion-dollar electronic computer gizmo or a new design for solar panels. Irrespective of the complexity of the technology, the need for research, experimentation, process of discovery, and prototyping is similar.

The lessons learned from this ad hoc project reiterate the importance of the following:

- Conduct research as needed and know the topic of interest well.
- Clearly understand the problem you are trying to solve.
- Put together a preliminary design that addresses key issues, answers key questions, and defines clear problem statements.
- Build prototypes and experiment with the prototypes to refine and adapt the design as needed.
- Reassess your project often to ensure you stay focused on solutions driven by the problem statements.
- Stay flexible, yet focused on problem solving to ensure your design is a good one.

Chapter 3: The Innovation Foundation, Birthplace of Ideas

In thinking about innovation, it is easy to jump to the conclusion that the definition for innovation is simply the same as invention. Well, not so fast. Let's break down these definitions further to establish a definition for both *invention* and *innovation*.

Given that the theme of this book is on establishing a framework for invention and innovation, it is important to define what is patentable. To establish this definition, we need to refer to United States Code (U.S.C.), Title 35 on Patents. 35 U.S.C. 101 provides the following definition: *"Whoever invents or discovers any new and useful process, machine, manufacture, or composition of matter, or any new and useful improvement thereof, may obtain a patent therefore, subject to the conditions and requirements of this title."*

Invention and the Inventor

For an invention to be considered for a patent, it must consist of both idea conception and reduction to practice. Reduction to practice with respect to a patent application covering your invention is the written specification and drawings that describe how someone with ordinary skill in the art of the invention could build the invention.

Thus, an individual can have an idea for an invention, but a patent cannot be applied for until the invention gets reduced to practice and described in enough detail such that a person with ordinary skill in the art covered by the invention can build it.

Your patent professional will write the patent application in a predefined format to be discussed later in this book; the sections in the application include a *detailed description*, *drawings,* and *claims* describing what you claim to be your invention. If you have developed prototypes, the prototypes will be helpful in writing the application and creating drawings to illustrate them. While prototypes are helpful, they are not required.

When someone tells you he or she thinks of hundreds of inventions every day, ask him or her if they can show you all the details of his or her inventions and a description covering how to build them. Coming up with (or conceiving) hundreds of ideas is one thing; inventing something that qualifies for a U.S. patent requires much more work and effort.

Invention Definition

Now let's define *invention* as it applies to the Creatively Inventing Framework:

An invention comprises novel solution(s) to one or more specific problems. When it is reduced to practice and can be described in detail, you can file for a U.S. patent.

Thus a problem can have many solutions, but when a *novel* solution is defined that has never been defined before, "Ah ha!" We have the moment of invention conception. Once we reduce the invention to practice such that a person with ordinary skill in the art of invention can build it, we can file for a patent on our invention.

The Process of Innovation

So what is innovation? I like to think of innovation as *the process* associated with the evolution of an idea into more ideas that may or may not result in a new product or patent application. It is very rare to have a new idea reduced to practice and deployed to the world as a new product without more ideas associated with the original idea occurring.

More often than not, one idea will generate another idea and another. I have established those "ah ha" moments in time, only to think of new ideas and additional content I wanted to add to a patent application after the patent application has already been filed with the USPTO. This is a common occurrence, and there are USPTO rules and regulations your patent professional can use to help you build onto your original invention with additional patent applications.

Innovation Definition

For the Creatively Inventing Framework, *innovation* is defined as follows:

Innovation is the process of starting with a problem and working to solve it while inventing solutions along the way.

Thus *innovation* may result in many new ideas that will become the content of one or more patent applications.

So how do you come up with the idea? The first two chapters helped answer that question.

Chapter 1 established Part I of the Creatively Inventing Framework using a question-asking process that evolved into a well-defined problem statement. Once the problem statement was defined, it could be broken down into elements, each of which was addressed by asking more questions and providing more answers until we finally refined the idea to a point where we could reduce it to practice.

In chapter 2, we developed the following problem statement once we understood our objective from a series of questions:

How can zucchini be grown in a confined area in a desert climate?

We decided that growing zucchini in a confined area was the problem we wanted to solve. Prototyping and experimenting were used to create solutions requiring adjustments along the way to ultimately define the final solution that became our invention: *A Vertical Growing Apparatus and Method.*

Filing Date

Another important detail to keep in mind is the filing date of the patent application. If another inventor were to have the same unique and novel idea as you did but filed a patent application one day after you filed yours, you would receive the patent and the other inventor would not. There are ways to handle such issues when an inventor in the United States can prove he or she conceived his or her invention and worked on it diligently before another inventor filed his or her patent application, but these are details to discuss with your patent professional, as such a scenario will depend on your specific situation.

The Patent Professional

I have worked with many patent professionals; a section on what to expect as an inventor or business is important to cover before we get too much further into the process.

While inventors could in theory submit their ideas to the patent office (USPTO) directly, the reality is that specific training on the expectations, rules and regulations, and process of the United States Patent and Trademark Office is essential; your patent application should be filed by a patent professional. Hiring a patent professional will give you the best chance of getting your invention allowed as a patent and include broad coverage and validity.

Who is a patent professional? Patent professionals[9] are individuals who have passed an examination (also known as the Patent Bar), administered by the USPTO, covering specific patent rules and regulations. Patent professionals fall into two categories:

---

9 You can look up a patent professional in your area via the USPTO website: https://oedci.uspto.gov/OEDCI/GeoRegion.jsp.

1. Patent attorneys
2. Patent agents

The patent attorney is an attorney with a technical background who has passed the USPTO Patent Bar examination. He or she are able to help you with the entire patent prosecution process, which includes patent application submission and interaction with the USPTO, and can also help you with legal matters such as licensing, legal opinions, litigation, and trademarks.

The patent agent, on the other hand, is an individual with a technical degree who has passed the Patent Bar examination, but is not an attorney and can only help you with patent application drafting, patent searches, and prosecution of your patent application with the USPTO.

Thus, if you are in need of legal advice beyond the patent rules and regulations of the USPTO, you should make sure that your patent professional is a patent attorney. For most inventors and companies, utilizing the services of a patent agent is a great option for obtaining a patent. Additionally, patent agents are often part of a law firm that includes patent attorneys who can help with your legal needs once you have been awarded a patent for your invention.

I also recommend requesting an estimate from the patent professional for each invention you wish to pursue. This will help to define the scope of the effort and associated budget in order to manage expenses. It will also help set expectations with the patent professional to stay within a budget established from his or her estimate.

Invention Disclosure Form

When you want to capture your idea initially or you are leading or working with a team and don't have full control or knowledge regarding all the details of a particular invention, it is best to use a form that can capture all of the key information related to the novel solution.

An Invention Disclosure Form is the approach used most often by larger companies and can also work nicely for the individual inventor. This form will include the key information your patent professional needs to do his or her job, and it will help you to capture all the important information before you forget the details associated with the solution. Note that there is no "one form fits all" for the Invention Disclosure Form, so the following is only an example and should be discussed with your patent professional to determine if any additional information is needed for your particular situation.

The example below captures the essential information required by the patent professional to do his or her job of working with the inventor to craft the patent application document that will be submitted to the USPTO.

1. Title of Invention

This section should include a brief descriptive title of the invention. The title included here may get changed later on by the patent professional, but is a good place to start.

2. Inventors

Include your full name and the name of any additional inventors and their contact information. To qualify as an inventor, the individuals listed must have contributed to at least part of the idea's conception.

For each inventor, list the following:

- Telephone number
- E-mail
- Address (this can come later, but will be needed once the idea becomes a patent application)

3. Problem Solved by Invention

This section should include as much detail as possible. The best information to be included within this section would be a problem statement that identifies the problem. The solution will go in another section of this form, so you should include the problem or market need solved by the invention.

If you are not able to articulate this in a short problem statement paragraph, then provide the information related to what caused the problem or why there was a need that caused you to think of a solution. Provide as much information as possible. Your patent professional may need to provide assistance later by creating a more detailed problem statement.

4. Previous Solutions or Closest Art

This section should describe the solutions available in the marketplace today that were available prior to your idea and solved the same (or a similar) problem. This could include any product information, Web site information, publications, patents, and patent applications that you believe represent the state of the art. This information is considered the prior art and should be fully disclosed.

5. Solution

This section should summarize your idea and include as much of a detailed description as possible covering the solution. This will be used as the source of information the patent professional will use to start the patent application and will aid the patent professional in establishing the date of conception of the invention. Additional information such as diagrams and flowcharts are always helpful and can be attached as stand-alone documents that are referenced in this section, even if the diagrams are rough sketches.

6. Differences/Advantages over the Current State of the Art

This section should include the differences between the invention and the currently available products or solutions. Another way to convey this is for you to provide as much information as possible on the current state of the art and why the new idea is better than other known solutions. What is it about the invention that makes it a better solution? Is it easier to build or manufacture? Does it do something unique? Is it lighter weight? Is the performance superior? Does it use less power or interact uniquely with the environment? Is it quicker or less expensive? Write down as much detail as possible.

7. Disclosures

This is a very critical section. Within the USPTO rules and regulations, there are specific time limits between the date the invention is disclosed to the public and the last possible date when a patent application can be filed. Discussions with the public may also include offers for sale at a trade show or to a customer. Any sales or presentations should also be identified. If there was a legal non-disclosure agreement in place as these presentations were made, that too is important and should be assessed by your patent professional (specifically your patent attorney). It is also important to identify the dates when the disclosure took place, even if it can only be estimated.

8. The Date When the Invention Was First Conceived or Realized

This should be the date of that "ah ha" moment when a solution was conceived to the identified problem, issue, or market opportunity. I've had many experiences during litigation where attorneys have asked me (the inventor) about that "ah ha" moment. What was I doing that led to the invention? What was my motivation? When did the first conception of the invention occur? So it is a good idea to write down notes that may be helpful to your patent professional later.

9. Inventor Signature

In this section, each inventor must sign and date the form. As with most legal documents, the patent professional may ask that the inventor use blue ink for his or her signature as it helps to identify the original.

______________________________ **Date:** ________________

Inventor 1

•

•

•

______________________________ **Date:** ________________

Inventor *N*

Inventor's Notebook

The inventor's notebook is a valuable tool for the inventor and for each member of a project team. The notebook provides you with a repository that can be used to keep track of the ideas you think of throughout a busy day.

Have you ever just had an idea pop into your mind and thought, *Hmm, I should write that one down*? But then you were sidetracked and later forgot the details of that "ah ha" moment?

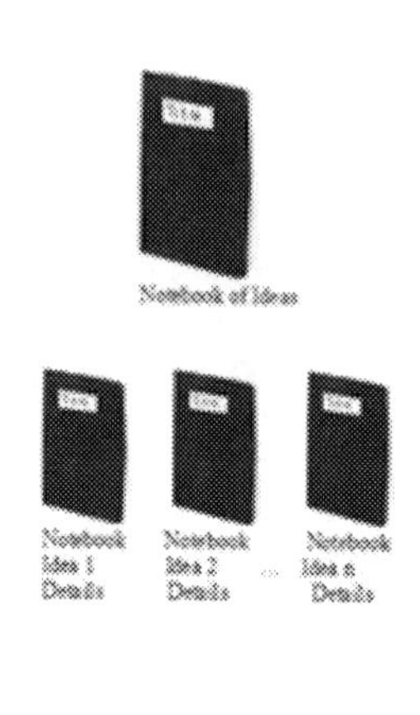

The inventor's notebook is the perfect repository for your ideas. There are other benefits too, besides the obvious benefit of capturing ideas. One of the key benefits is that such a notebook provides proof of when the invention was conceived and what was done to reduce it to practice. These dates can be extremely important if there is ever a challenge regarding who created an idea first. Your patent attorney should address the legal implications with you as it relates to your specific business situation.

From my experience, the inventor's notebook is one of those handy journal devices that help me remember ideas that pop into my head. Generally, such a notebook should have pages permanently affixed to the binding such that pages *cannot* be removed or replaced. The pages can be blank or lined, but should include the information shown above as a guideline in the Inventor's Notebook Page example.

Some of the basic items to include on each page of the notebook are the following:

- Idea name or project name
- Date
- Text of information related to your idea
- Drawings of your idea

- Your name, signature, and date
- A witness name, signature, and date

You may even try to include most if not all of the sections defined in the Information Disclosure Form we described above.

Clearly, finding a witness to sign every page can get to be a bit of an inconvenience. So you may want to periodically have someone review your notebook and write a little statement in your notebook that he or she reviewed the ideas on pages *x* to *y*, and then have him or her sign and date it.

If you are like me with lots of ideas and projects going, you may wish to use a systematic approach for logging your ideas. The best way to do this is to have a master idea notebook that captures the main ideas and then use an additional notebook for the details related to one specific project. This way, if you ever have to go back and prove when you came up with the idea and what you did to reduce it to practice, you will have documentation in a single notebook.

As indicated earlier, it is best to discuss the details of your specific situation with your patent professional so he or she can advise you. However, the information presented in this section should give you a starting point.

For team leaders who wish to provide a standard process for all of their team members, issuing a company-provided inventor's notebook is the best way to go. There are numerous suppliers of inventor's notebooks that can be found online. If you Google "Inventor's Notebook," you will have a list of Web sites that provide these notebooks. You might also check the Web site associated with this book, as we list some additional options for your consideration: www.thinktekglobally.com.

The team should be encouraged to use these notebooks as they write their notes and ideas down for a particular project. I often get asked if I recommend a specific inventor's notebook for a company to use. With half the battle being to get your team members to write information down, I recommend keeping the process simple so they will in fact use them. The team members should capture the basic information in their notebooks throughout the workday, and the team leader can review their notebooks periodically. The team leader can even periodically provide the witness review of their ideas.

Example: The Self-Contained Automatic Watering System

Using the following green-tech, consumer-oriented product example, developed by a team of inventors in Florida, the process of innovation will be demonstrated, including a patent application that was developed to describe the invention, which was issued a U.S. patent.

Thinking back on the pet toy example and the process used to develop the problem statement, you should now understand how you would work toward the development of new products using research and asking a lot of questions. So rather than going through the same research process, let's start this example with a problem statement we want to solve.

Problem Statement Detail:

How can a range of stationary houseplants be automatically and sufficiently watered for extended periods of time?

Who hasn't had this problem? If you like plants that are living rather than the silk, dust-collecting variety, you can relate to this problem. So the first step in the process will be to research the prior art or products available for solving this problem.

We do numerous searches on the Internet and find a number of products available today. One solution is a large water container with multiple tubes to water plants. A consumer gathers all his or her houseplants and places them in a common area where the water container is located.

While this sounds like a solution, it also sounds inconvenient. Who wants to move plants around every time they go on vacation or go on a business trip? Most folks I know are in a mad rush before a trip out of town, and taking time to move around plants would probably be pretty low on the pretrip to-do list.

We find other products such as glass water bulbs that distribute water directly into the plant's container as the plant needs water. The only problem with this solution is how to determine the number of glass bulbs to use to thoroughly water each plant and ensure enough water is distributed to the entire root system of the plant.

There is another solution that works using the process of transference, where water is drawn from a water container to a plant container using strings, like a candle's wick. Again, the problem with this solution is ensuring the plant's root system gets enough water.

With an understanding now of the prior art, we start to think about a solution that can water the plant thoroughly, perhaps even water the plant at a regularly scheduled time with a predetermined amount of water. Now, we have some parameters for how we should solve the problem. Let's recap where we are:

Problem Statement: How can a range of stationary houseplants be automatically and sufficiently watered for extended periods of time?

Solution parameters (also known as requirements):

- Plant needs to be watered thoroughly
- Plant needs to be watered periodically
- Plant should not need to be relocated
- Watering should be flexible to support different sized plants
- Water should be stored in a reservoir to be refilled once a month or thereabouts

An interesting benefit to a solution with these parameters is that a consumer would never need to manually water his or her plants again. That would be a cool product!

Now, let's work on visualizing what such a product would look like.

First, since houseplants are grown in containers, it makes sense to build a container with the desired solution requirements. Second, let's describe the container we are creating. We can start by making a list:

1. A container with a space to hold water that is separate from the space where the soil for the plant resides
2. A pump with a battery power source that can transfer water from the reservoir into the space holding the soil for the plant

3. A timer with a battery power source, integrated with the pump, that allows the consumer to set the watering time as either daily, every two days, every three days, or every seven days
4. A program that allows a consumer to determine how long the pump will remain engaged to control the amount of water distributed to the plant

We integrate these features into a single plant container product, and "Ah ha!" Now we have our invention conception. Next, we start to visualize the features described on this list as a product that we can build. That's right; we are reducing it to practice in a constructive way—on paper.

We imagine a plastic container that will hold our plant. The reservoir will encircle the space where the plant will reside, and the pump will fit right down into the reservoir nice and secure, to ensure water doesn't splash out of the reservoir. The pump will distribute water from the reservoir through a tube extending above the plant and stream water onto our plant.

I've got a nice image in my mind and have written it down in my inventor's notebook. Cool! This is fun, isn't it?

Next let's innovate a bit. Thinking about the pump for a moment, the water will stream through the tube and land on a fixed point of soil associated with our plant. Such a solution may not actually water the entire plant if the water streams out to a single point of soil associated with the plant.

What if we place a spray-like tip on the end of our watering tube so it delivers water out in a fine spray onto the soil of our plant? Sure that would be better, but it still doesn't water around the entire perimeter of the plant.

What if we pump water into the tube *and* also direct water sideways around a plastic rim on the top of the container? The plastic rim would need evenly spaced openings to allow water to move onto the plant around the edge of the soil associated with the plant. This design would provide both a stream of water from above the plant and a stream of water around the plastic rim of the plant container that would flow down onto the edge of the soil around the plant.

That sounds a bit complicated, but with plastics and plastic molds, it should not be a problem. Next step, we start to prototype the product. As we are prototyping the product, we will want to make sure all of our notes are written up so we can get them to our patent professional to start working on patent protection for us. We can use the format from the Invention Disclosure Form we discussed earlier.

Here is how the product turned out and how the patent application was written:

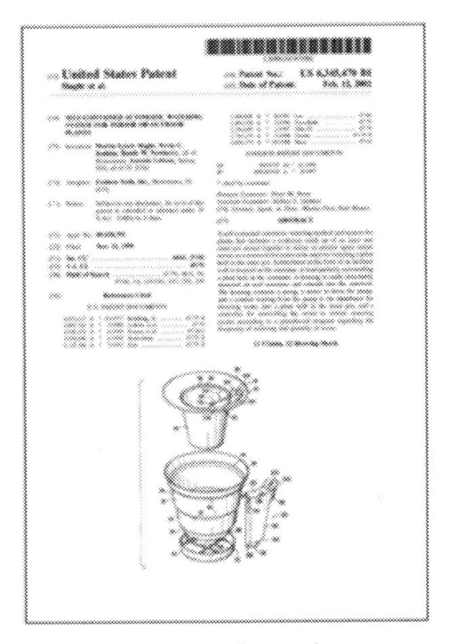

Here is the description summary from the patent:

It is the principal object of the present invention to supply to the marketplace a watering system for potted plants that overcomes the drawbacks and disadvantages of the prior art, and will be simple to use, simple to service, and relatively inexpensive and, therefore, affordable. This object is accomplished by the provision of a system that utilizes a nested pot arrangement, with a reservoir defined in the annular space between an outer pot and an inner pot. The inner pot serves as a container for the plant. The novel system of the present invention includes a unique delivery of water from the reservoir to distribute water to the plant circumferentially, at the outer perimeter of the plant's root system, as well as directing water into the base of the plant or foliage of the plant. The novel system provides an electronic control of the water delivery to enable the quantity, frequency, and timing to be selected by the plant owner and, thereby, tailors the water delivery to the needs of the plant, even when the plant owner is unavailable or absent for prolonged periods of time. Further, the operating components are contained in a modular housing so that it can be readily removed for repair or servicing or returned for factory servicing while replaced with a new housing.

Other and further objects and advantages of the present invention will become apparent from the following detailed description of a preferred embodiment of the invention when taken with the appended drawings.

Here are the claims that were allowed by the USPTO (yes, that means this invention received a U.S. patent):

What is claimed is:

1. A self-contained automatic watering system for plants comprising:

    a container open at the top,

    a distributor mounted adjacent to the open top of the container extending at least partially around the periphery of the container,

    a water reservoir,

    a housing extending into said reservoir, said housing containing a pump located in said reservoir, a motor to drive said pump, and a conduit leading from the pump to the distributor for directing water peripherally onto the distributor, and

    a controller for controlling the motor to initiate watering cycles according to a preselected program regarding the frequency of watering and quantity of water.

2. A self-contained automatic watering system for plants comprising:

    a container open at its top comprised of an inner and

outer pot nested to define an annular space there between to serve as a reservoir for water to be used for watering a plant held in the inner pot,

a distributor mounted adjacent to the opening at the top of the container extending at least partially around the periphery of the container,

a housing easily detachable mounted on said container and extending into the annular space, said housing containing a pump having an inlet and outlet located in said annular space, a motor to drive said pump, and a conduit leading from the pump outlet to the distributor for directing water peripherally onto the distributor, and

a controller for controlling the motor to initiate watering cycles according to a preselected program regarding the frequency of watering and quantity of water.

3. A watering system according to claim 2 wherein the distributor includes an inclined wall.
4. A watering system according to claim 2 wherein said housing is easily detachable mounted in said container.
5. A watering system according to claim 2 wherein said conduit terminates in a tee having two branches, one to direct water from the reservoir peripherally around the distributor and the other to direct water radially into the container.
6. A watering system according to claim 2 wherein the housing defines two compartments, one containing the motor and pump and the other containing the controller.
7. A watering system according to claim 2 wherein an audible indicator is provided that is controlled by the controller.
8. A watering system according to claim 2 wherein a visual indicator is provided that is controlled by the controller.
9. A watering system according to claim 2 wherein a means is provided to detect the presence of water in the reservoir.
10. A watering system according to claim 2 wherein a power level sensor is provided that provides a signal to the controller.

11. A watering system according to claim 2 wherein the controller is provided with input keys.
12. A watering system according to claim 11 wherein the input keys include a key for inputting a delay into the controller, a key for inputting the quantity of water to be delivered to the plant, and a key for inputting the frequency of delivery of water.
13. A watering system according to claim 1 wherein the housing is divided into three parts, an upper part, a lower part, and an intermediate part.

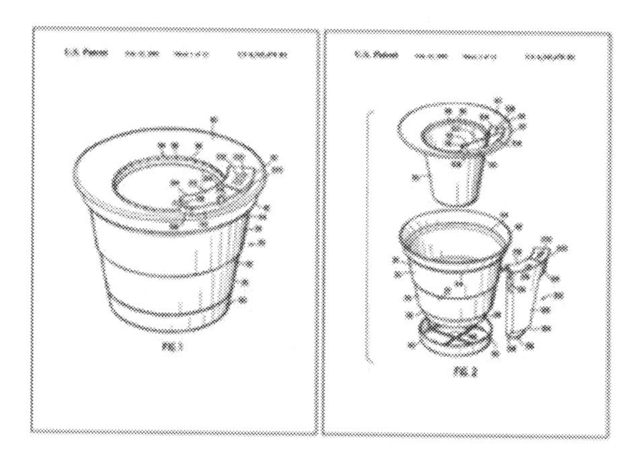

While the product shown above is pretty cool and solves our current problem, there is a bigger problem to solve for those of us with many plants in our home. How do we solve the challenge of watering plants throughout a location, such as an entire home, apartment, or office?

Example: Plant Watering System

Problem statement: It is time consuming and inconvenient to manually water multiple plants throughout an office or home.

We could further add to our earlier invention to provide a new solution that would minimize the programming time and maintenance associated with many individual plant containers within an office or home. So what sort of solution could we dream up to solve this problem?

Let's break down the issue:

- A plant container for each plant
  - * To make this concept feasible and worthwhile, we could make the assumption that a consumer could use the previous single plant container invention when they have six plants or fewer in their office or home.
  - * A consumer survey or trial could validate this assumption. If it takes one minute to configure each plant container using our earlier invention, six plant containers would take six minutes. Taking longer than six minutes would make our earlier invention frustrating for most consumers.
  - * Thus if it takes two minutes to configure up to twenty-five plant containers using our new invention, consumers would find the time savings desirable.
- Each plant container includes a reservoir with a programmable pump using a battery source
- Each plant container needs to be periodically monitored to determine if it is working
- Plant containers could be located one or more rooms apart
- Plants are to be watered
- Plants may be periodically fertilized using liquid fertilizer

What sort of fundamental technologies can we use to provide our unique product and application? What about computer networking? That is, we could place each plant container on a network where the electronics associated with each container's pump could also include computer network electronics.

Thinking about this more, I imagine wires running throughout my house to each container. What a mess! But wait, we could use wireless network technology in each plant container, where all the plant containers are connected to a single controller. "Ah ha!" This is starting to make sense now.

The single computer network controller can provide a single access point for the consumer to program each and every container throughout the home or business location. It could even include a health check for each container to verify the container is operating properly. If there were a container with a malfunction, the health check would report the issue back to the central controller over the wireless network and report the specific plant container with the malfunction.

Now, this is starting to sound really cool. I could control a bunch of plant containers from a single location in my home to program the amount of water and time interval for each of the plant containers, which may be different depending on the variety of plants within the location.

Let's compile the information into an Invention Disclosure Form and include as many features as we can think of just as we discussed earlier. Not to worry, there will be more time to add additional features and functionality as you work with your patent professional. However, the information you provide that follows will expedite the overall translation of your idea into a patent application by the patent professional.

Example: Invention Disclosure Form

1. Title of Invention

Plant Watering System

2. Inventors

Rick Rowe, telephone, e-mail, and address information

3. Problem Solved by Invention

It is time consuming and inconvenient to manually water multiple plants throughout an office or home.

4. Previous Solutions or Closest Art

- *Gardening is a very popular pastime. In urban environments and indoors, gardening is often limited to growing potted plants. Unfortunately, there are several drawbacks or problems associated with growing and tending potted plants.*
- *The most significant problem in tending to potted plants is watering and feeding them. Generally, the gardener must individually tend to each potted plant, determining when to*

water and feed them and how much water and food to provide to each plant. Plants of different types may require different amounts of water or water at different intervals. Whether of the same or a different type, plants located in sunny versus shaded areas or located in different types or sizes of pots may all have different levels of water usage. Thus, a gardener may need to tend various plants on an everyday basis, watering and feeding different plants on different days. Even this difficult tending process requires the presence of the gardener. Thus, when a homeowner leaves his or her home for a period of time, such as for a vacation, the homeowner must find another party to tend to the plants or else they may die.

- *Various solutions have been proposed to these problems. In the case of outdoor plants, automated irrigation systems are known. These systems generally utilize pipes to deliver water from a source to a sprinkler head or the like, from which the water is dispensed. A timer is configured to turn valves on and off, thus controlling the flow of water through the pipes.*
- *This type of system, however, is not well suited to use in supplying water to indoor plants. First, the normal irrigation system is configured to deliver water to a number of points using a common delivery pipe. For example, multiple sprinkler heads for watering a large area are supplied water using a single delivery pipe. This configuration does not work with indoor plants, where each plant needs to be provided a unique amount of water at unique watering schedules.*
- *In addition, these irrigation systems are dependent upon a network of connected pipes to deliver water. In the outdoor environment, these pipes can be run underground so as to not be visible and to avoid their being an obstacle. Again, this configuration is not well suited to the indoor/house environment. Pipes cannot be conveniently run about a house. Aside from the fact the pipes can't be readily be buried and are thus unsightly and interfere with use of the home, house plants may be moved about and may be located in various positions, including by hanging them.*

5. Solution

- *The invention is a plant watering system and a method of watering one or more plants. The invention applies to watering indoor, potted plants.*
- *The system includes a main controller and one or more watering devices. Each watering device includes a reservoir capable of containing water to be delivered to one or more plants, a conduit leading from the reservoir to an outlet from which the water is dispensed to the plants, and an electronically controlled flow controller controlling the flow of water from the reservoir through the conduit to the outlet. The main controller includes at least one user input and a controller configured to generate watering device control signals. The watering device control signals can be transmitted wirelessly from the main controller to each watering device.*
- *The reservoir is located in a body which is configured as a statue or the watering device controller and other components may also be located in the plant container, where the watering device is configured as a portable, stand-alone device. A conduit, such as a tube or pipe, leads from the reservoir to the outlet. The flow controller can be a pump which draws fluid from the reservoir, or a valve which controls the flow of fluid from the reservoir.*
- *The system may include one or more moisture sensors. The sensors may be placed in the soil of the plant that is being watered. A sensor can be associated with a particular watering device. Moisture sensor data is provided by the watering device back to the main controller, where it may be used to adjust water delivery or generate a warning.*
- *The main controller can include a display, such as a touch sensitive display, used to display watering information. The information may include graphical information regarding the watering devices, including their relative locations (such as mapped to a house floor plan). The main controller can also include a data storage device for storing user-inputted information, generated watering information (such as watering start times and water durations), as well as pre-programmed watering schedules. A user may input information regarding a*

plant to be watered, such as pot size, soil type, plant size, and/or plant characteristic, which information is used to generate the watering schedule for a particular plant.

- *The main controller can be configured to transmit "water on" commands or instructions to each watering device at the appropriate times. The watering devices then control the flow controllers to permit water to flow to the plant(s). When the watering time is over, the main controller sends a signal to the watering device to shut off the flow of water. The program information may be transmitted to a controller of the watering device, and the watering device may generate such signals and locally control the flow controller. After initial programming, communication with the main controller is not required in order for the watering strategy to be implemented.*

  The watering devices may include a flow controller automatic shut-off. The shut-off may be used to ensure water flow at each watering device is shut off in the event the communication link is lost.

6. Differences/Advantages over the Current State of the Art

Some solutions particular to potted plants have been proposed. For example, one proposed solution is to provide potted plants with a bowl or tray which can be filled with water. Water is drawn or "wicked" by the soil up from the bowl to the potted plant. Unfortunately, this solution does not address individual plant watering requirements, especially relative to plants which are best-suited to infrequent watering.

7. Disclosures

This invention has been developed within Think Tek's idea lab in Las Vegas and no disclosure to anyone has occurred. (Note: Since I have actually already submitted this invention as a U.S. patent application, this is only an example of what you would write if you had just developed the idea. Obviously, by including it in this book, I am disclosing it to the public too. So beware of what you disclose to the public before you submit the patent application.)

8. When was the invention first conceived or realized?

On mm/dd/yyyy I came up with the idea. (Remember, this should be the date of your "ah ha" moment when you came up with the solution above.)

9. Inventor signature(s):

Rick Rowe – mm/dd/yyyy

Here is only a portion of patent application that was eventually submitted:

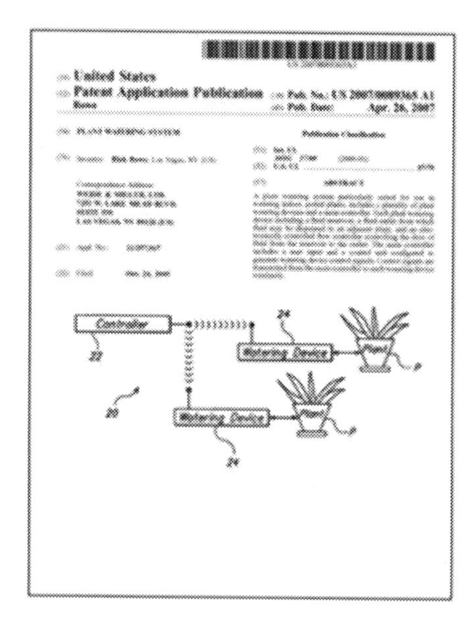

United States
Patent Application Publication

Controller
Watering Device
Watering Device

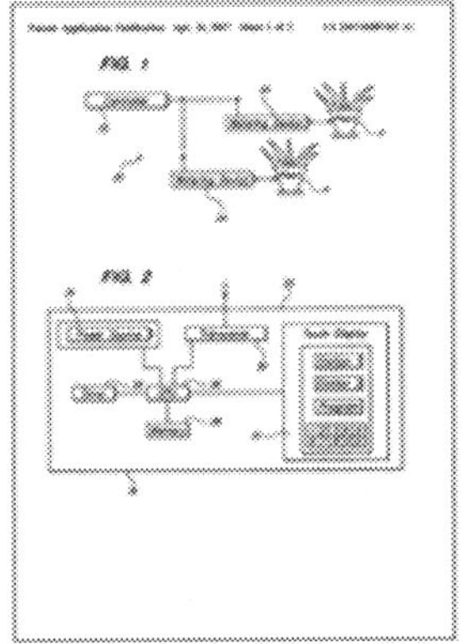
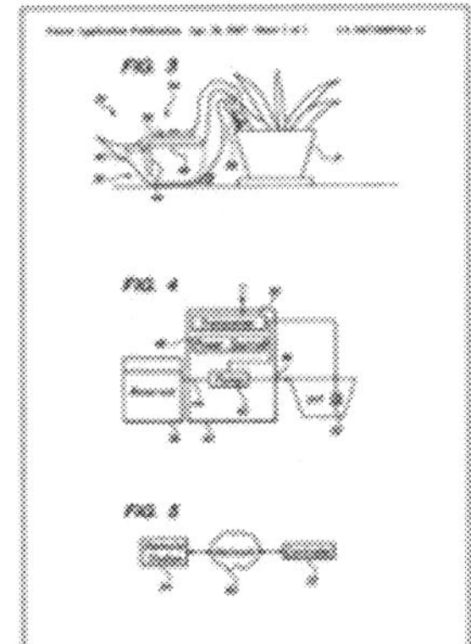

Description of the Drawings

- Figure 1 illustrates a plant watering system in accordance with an embodiment of the invention.
- Figure 2 schematically illustrates one embodiment of a main controller of a plant watering system in accordance with the invention.
- Figure 3 illustrates a watering device and associated plant of a plant watering system of the invention.
- Figure 4 schematically illustrates one embodiment of a watering device of a system of the invention.
- Figure 5 schematically illustrates a second embodiment of a communication configuration for a system of the invention.

Detailed Description Of The Invention

The invention is a method and system for watering one or more plants. In the following description, numerous specific details are set forth in order to provide a more thorough description of the present invention. It will be apparent, however, to one skilled in the art, that the present invention may be practiced without these specific details. In other instances, well-known features have not been described in detail so as not to obscure the invention.

In general, the invention is a plant watering system and a method of watering one or more plants. In one embodiment, the system includes a main controller which communicates with individual watering devices. Each watering device includes at least one water reservoir from which water is drawn and delivered to a plant …

(Note: The above paragraph is only the first paragraph of a multipage detailed description where each reference point identified in the figures above is referenced and explained to the level required for someone to build your invention.)

Claims

1. A plant watering system comprising:

    a plurality of plant watering devices, each plant watering device including a reservoir capable of containing fluid to be delivered to one or more plants, a conduit leading from said reservoir to an outlet from which said fluid is dispensed to said one or more plants, an electronically controlled flow controller controlling the flow of fluid from said reservoir through said conduit to said outlet, and a receiver configured to receive wireless control instructions and provide electronic signals to said flow controller; and

    a main controller including at least one user input, a data storage device configured to store watering device control data, a control unit configured to generate watering device control signals based upon said control data, and a transmitter configured to transmit control signals over one or more wireless communication links to said plant watering devices.

    …

    Note: Only the first "applied for" claim is identified above to give you a general idea of how this came out.

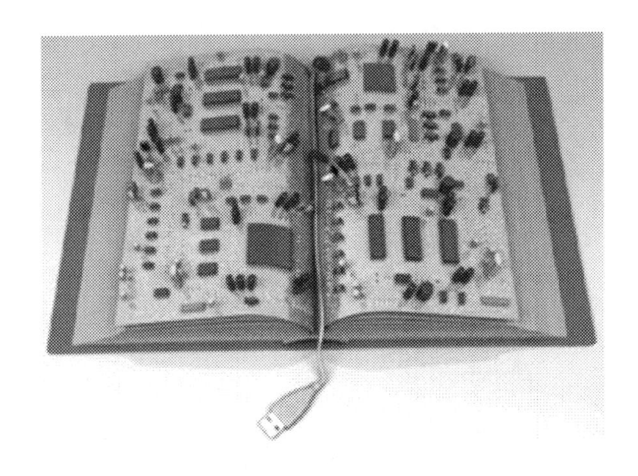

Chapter 4: Inspirational Innovation and the "Ah Ha" Moment

How does one become inspired to innovate and invent? How does inspiration help in the formation of new ideas?

I have talked to many inventors; oftentimes, they were inspired because they saw a better way, were bothered by something, or were determined to solve a particular problem. There are other common traits that motivate inventors, such as the insatiable desire to solve a problem along with an obsession to make it better by continuously moving from one solution that doesn't work to another that might work, until a solution is finally found.

Passion and Curiosity

Most inventors I know are alive with the passion to creatively solve problems. After all, isn't inventing simply creating something new? Solving a problem using a new method? Looking at the world differently from others? Looking at the world we live in as if we were experiencing it for the first time?

Now wait a minute. "Looking at the world we live in as if we were experiencing it for the first time." What do I mean by that?

Let's think deeper about that for a moment. Could that be why my young daughter asked, "Why is the sky blue?" She may have been curious about the world, or perhaps for the first time, she was looking at the world beyond herself and her immediate surroundings.

So in trying to frame the concept of inspiration with respect to invention, couldn't we define inspiration as an insatiable curiosity that drives a passionate motivation to creatively solve problems?

So how does one get that light bulb to go on inside his or her head and become inspired? I suppose the question is almost as fun to answer as "Why is the sky blue?" It is a good question, and if we could package up the answer, we might have something pretty valuable.

Unfortunately, from my experience there is no one simple answer to that question. Inspiration comes when you least expect it and, most certainly, never when you are trying to force it. However, you can create a framework to cultivate inspiration. For me, I get inspired when I listen to a great inventor talk about how he or she came up with an incredible invention, or when I listen to an artist sing like there is no tomorrow, or when I watch the sunrise from the shore of a high mountain lake.

When I feel driven to solve a problem, and an idea on how to solve it comes to me, or when that light goes on in my head and I know the solution to a nagging problem, those are the moments that motivate and excite me. I imagine most people feel similar excitement when they get inspired and then solve a problem. So what makes inventors different?

Most inventors I have known act on that little voice or gut feeling. Inventors hear the voice and listen to it; they start asking questions and interacting with the voice and become obsessively inspired to solve a problem by creating something new and unique. Sometimes, their unique solutions can be perceived as very different.

How do I know this? Another simple question; that's what happens to me personally and to most of the inventors I have known. That is probably why many inventors I know have been called "out there" at one point or another in their business life. That is, their new and unique solutions may not be fully appreciated … yet.

We inventors act on those moments when we see something and want to make it better or notice a problem and must solve it. We create our own version of the future by connecting and applying bits of information, technology, and ideas in a unique way that no one has ever done before.

An inspired inventor becomes creative and ignores the traditional boundaries everyone else in the world lives within. For example, I wonder how people perceived the notion of Edison's light bulb during Edison's time? I suspect many thought he was pretty out there. After all, candlelight and oil lamps seemed to work pretty well.

Inspiration Triggers

Each of us has different triggers for inspiration. Triggers can come in the form of a beautiful sunset, early morning on a high mountain lake, inspirational words from a world leader, a smile from your child, a world-class performance from a famous musician, and so on.

The list is almost endless. The challenge for most of us is finding the time to reflect on these moments to help excite and motivate us to transform the present moment into an inspirational moment.

When we are able to make time to enjoy such a moment, we remember it forever. So why not make more of those moments in your life inspirational moments?

Moments that inspire us to think bigger than ourselves, moments that inspire us to help others, and moments that inspire us to solve the unsolvable and see opportunity everywhere: these are the moments that get us excited and make life energizing and fun.

Example: Golf Cart Method and Apparatus

Most everyone I know has been inspired by watching a talented pro golfer perform his or her magic on the golf course. Watching him or her hit the golf ball so accurately and with so much power is absolutely amazing.

While thinking about golf one day and participating in a golf tournament, my friend Stephen Moore from Las Vegas had a great idea. He noticed that most golf carts are painted with sponsorship information or have labels stuck to the cart in odd places to highlight the sponsors.

He started thinking, "What if there was a way to create a plastic mold that fit precisely over the front of the golf cart?" The plastic mold could then be painted and modified with sponsorship and event information and could later be recycled. This way, the original golf cart would remain intact and a new mold could be created for each upcoming event.

Here are a few of the key information areas of the Invention Disclosure Form associated with this idea:

Title of Invention

Method and Apparatus for Customizing a Golf Cart

Background

Motorized golf carts are commonly used to transport golfers and their golf clubs during the play of golf. A variety of different configurations of golf carts are known. Some carts are electrically powered, while others use a gas motor. Some carts seat two players, while others seat four.

Generally, all golf carts have a body or shell that extends over the drive elements of the cart. The body is often constructed of fiberglass or similar durable material.

Manufacturers of these golf carts generally make generic styles or models of golf carts. Often, the golf carts are painted a standard white, while in some instances a particular style may be painted red, green, or another color. In most instances, however, each golf cart is essentially the same and indistinguishable from every other golf cart of a particular model or style.

Users of golf carts, including individuals and golf courses, however, often desire to "personalize" the golf carts. For example, a golf course may purchase fifty golf carts for use by its members. The golf course may have a third party paint a logo or apply stickered letters to the body of the golf cart, such as to designate the golf carts as property of the golf course. Individual cart owners may do the same, such as to enable them to distinguish their cart from others' carts.

These methods of "personalizing" the carts, however, have various drawbacks. In general, these methods result in permanent modification to the carts. This lessens the value of the carts to others, such as when an individual wishes to sell his or her golf cart. In addition, the particular customization prevents use of the cart for other purposes. For example, a golf course may have their logo painted on each cart. If a tournament organizer wishes to conduct a tournament at that course, the organizer may desire that the carts bear the tournament name, rather than the course name.

A convenient method of personalizing one or more golf carts is desired.

Summary

The invention is a method and apparatus for customizing or personalizing a golf cart.

One configuration of the invention is a media display for a golf cart. The media display preferably comprises a body having a top side or surface and a bottom side or surface. Media is associated with the body. The media may comprise coloring, lettering, numbering, or art or graphics, such as logos. The media may be associated with the top and/or bottom sides, or be located within the body.

In one configuration, the body is generally rigid, such as by being constructed of molded or formed plastic, acrylic, or fiberglass. The body may have various configurations, including shapes and sizes. Preferably, the body is configured to fit on or over at least a portion of the front or forward portion of a golf cart. In one configuration, the body is generic in configuration for mating with golf carts of various configurations. In another embodiment, the body has a particular configuration for mating with a particular style or configuration of golf cart. For example, in one configuration the body may be generally rectangular in shape for location over the front of any golf cart having sufficient area for accepting the display. In another configuration, the body may be configured to include headlight or bumper cut-outs and/or be molded to conform to the front of a particularly styled golf cart having headlights and front area of various elevations/slopes.

Functionality is provided for connecting one or more media displays to a golf cart. In a preferred configuration, the functionality permits a media display to be selectively connected to a golf cart, thus facilitating both ease of connection and disconnection from a golf cart. In one configuration, the functionality comprises mating hook and loop material, threaded fasteners, or the like.

In accordance with a method of the invention, a golf cart is customized or personalized by associating a media display with the golf cart. Preferably, the media display exhibits particular media and is located at the front or forward portion of the golf cart. Association of the media display with the golf cart permits the golf cart to be customized to bear particular logos, text, or the like. Further, the media display may be modified, such as to display other media, or a replacement media display may be connected to the golf cart in order to change the configuration of the cart.

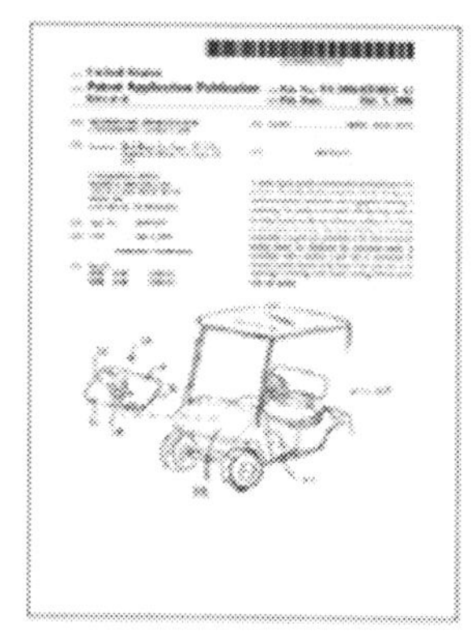

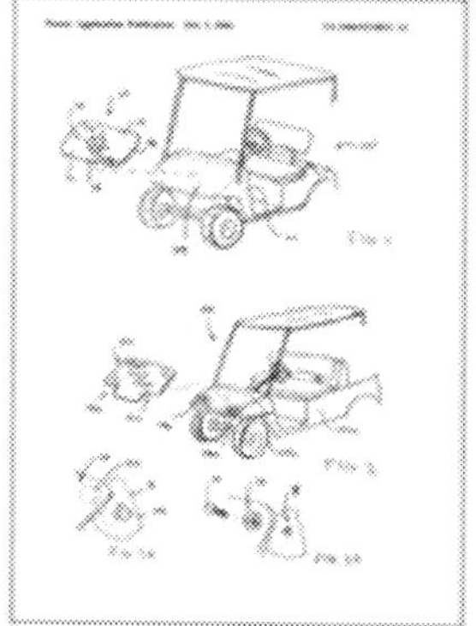

This golf cart invention example demonstrates that even in an existing popular sport like golfing, there is always room for innovation. A footnote to this story: We ultimately decided not to pursue this particular patent application after we reviewed the prior art that the USPTO identified in an Office Action rejecting all our claims as being obvious.

Doesn't this contradict the notion that there is always room for innovation? Not at all, but it does mean you may not be able to obtain a patent on all your innovations. Unfortunately, this is an important part of the patent process many inventors learn the hard way. No matter how much research you do, there still may exist prior art that prevents you from obtaining a patent on the claims of your invention. So while our initial research in the market indicated there was opportunity, the USPTO found prior art they felt made our invention obvious and rejected our claims.

Thus, you must take a look at the USPTO issues raised in Office Actions and decide if it is worth the expense of responding to the USPTO. With a well-written patent application with plenty of detail, we did have options, including pursuing the patent by filing new claims, further responding to the USPTO with a solid argument that our original claims were novel, or deciding to pursue the innovation without applying for a patent.

Part II: Three-Step Inspiration Boost

Now, let's summarize the process presented in this chapter into Part II of the Creatively Inventing Framework: the "Three-Step Inspiration Boost." It will help motivate you to get into the proper mind-set for inventing and problem solving.

1. Clear the present moment
   Think of a problem that you wish to solve and then clear your head of all the daily noise and relax.

2. Reflect
   Reflect on those moments when you have felt inspired.

3. Switch to the present moment and think of solutions
   Now, move back to the present moment and think of the problem you are trying to solve and solve it.

Chapter 5: Go, Team, Go: Innovation Strategy for Teams

A common question that often comes up when I am working with companies relates to implementing an innovation strategy effort for teams. As such, this chapter will focus on using a team of inventors to innovate and develop an intellectual property strategy. However, individual inventors may also find the information useful as well.

Once the team gets into the mode of generating ideas, how should the ideas be sorted to identify which ideas to develop or focus on? How should ideas be selected from a long list of ideas for development into patent applications?

Clearly, the examples we have previously discussed, such as the pet toy example, used a systematic process to identify a consumer need and relate that need to the development of a new product. That process worked nicely for the pet toy example, where there was a clear goal in mind. However, oftentimes a team of inventors or a company may want to broaden the net of possible opportunity by leveraging the knowledge and experience of their team to brainstorm the creation of new products or product enhancements.

Brainstorming

Brainstorming[10]—where questions are asked and ideas are generated while a facilitator writes ideas down—is a well-known technique that can be used as part of an innovation strategy. There have been many books written on the subject of brainstorming, so the focus of this section will be to reinforce how questions can be used to generate ideas (answers) and how those results can be organized into an innovation strategy.

When you have a group participating in the process, you will need one or two people acting as facilitators to ask the questions and encourage the team to generate more ideas. For a smaller group, those participating may simply need to take on both the facilitator and idea team member roles during the process.

In a team environment, the questions these facilitators ask should be well thought out ahead of time so the team can focus on generating answers during the brainstorming session. For companies using these techniques, I recommend that the facilitators discuss these questions with the executive management team prior to the sessions to establish some degree of focus for the team participating and to establish buy-in from the executive management team.

Why is this so important? Remember, you will need to allocate time and resources for this effort in addition to patent professional resources. All of that will translate into an expense to the company, resulting in the executive management team expecting a return on the company's investment.

To get the process started, here are some questions the facilitator can ask the team:

- What do customers like about the current products?
- What do customers dislike about the current products?

10 An interesting brainstorming reference: www.effectivemeetings.com/teams/participation/brainstorming.asp.

- What needs have customers raised that can be provided by enhancing or modifying current products?
- What needs have your customers raised that can be translated into new products?
- What are your ideas for new products?
- What are your ideas for new product features or capabilities?

The series of questions used by the facilitators, such as the examples above, should generate a large number of ideas from the team. There is also an additional dimension I highly recommend to the groups I work with that goes beyond the traditional brainstorming methodology. I suggest establishing multiple time frames. Then have the facilitator ask the same questions *in each of the desired time frames.*

1. **Short-term:** within two years (tactical)
   The short-term time frame should represent more of an immediate need. Since the process of applying for a patent may take three to five years, this time frame may not result in ideas your team will develop into patent applications. However, there may be ideas that have long-term impact that you will want to protect by applying for patent protection, or there may be enhancements you will want to make to existing products without applying for a patent. As such, these will be business decisions with respect to the amount of money you or your company is willing to spend on patent applications.

2. **Medium-term:** within five years (strategic)
   The medium-term time frame will be where most of the team will feel comfortable generating ideas, since it is generally not a stretch to imagine where the business or business opportunities may be within five years. It also helps keep the ideas somewhat grounded and focused on products for which the management team can easily understand the business opportunity. As such, this will most likely be where the majority of the resources will be allocated for intellectual property development efforts.

3. **Long-term:** over five years (strategic)
   The long-term time frame will be the most difficult for the majority of teams to imagine. Many times, an action-oriented team will consider this time frame as too much dreaming and not based in reality. But I have found this is the time frame that gets the team thinking beyond their "today mentality." When you press for the team to think this far out, they will generate ideas that are indeed too far outside the box, but some ideas may surprise you. These are the ideas we are really trying to get the team to come up with during this process.

The team will have a chance to participate in prioritizing their ideas, so those that are way outside the box will be prioritized lower. Also remember that patent protection covers twenty years from the filing or priority date of the patent, so this long-term time frame is worth exploring with the team.

The answers to the questions asked by the facilitators for each of the time frames may or may not be different when the team starts throwing out ideas. To ensure the team puts their minds into the proper time frames, the facilitators need to remind the group to focus their minds on the desired time frame by thinking of answers to the questions while visualizing how the world (or your business environment) will look in the time frame identified. The facilitators may even give some examples of how the business environment might look to get the team thinking in the mind-set.

For example, what new technologies may be developed that your products can leverage? What might be the focus of the marketplace in each of the time frames? How might your customers change in each of the time frames? What new opportunities might there be? Thus we will want to prioritize the ideas the team generates into two or three time periods depending on how many time frames are meaningful.

Once the team has generated a large list of ideas, trying to prioritize these ideas can become very challenging. To make this process of prioritizing ideas more efficient, the ideas will be organized into groups of opportunity or idea categories.

Part III: Seven-Step Strategic Planning Process

Let's now define Part III of Creatively Inventing Framework, where the ideas identified in the brainstorming session are organized into a prioritized list used to focus both intellectual property development and product development resources.

This process will result in a focused approach in which your team or company can apply resources and efforts to develop or enhance products. Additionally, the process of intellectual property development (patenting your ideas) should be closely coupled to the focus and priority of product development.

Once ideas have been articulated, the team should identify between five and ten idea categories, or more if appropriate, in which the ideas generated during the brainstorming effort can be grouped. These idea categories should be given titles that capture the theme of a group of ideas. For example, idea categories can be broadly defined, such as applications, infrastructure, devices, interfaces, and databases.

Idea categories may also be specific product categories such as in our previous example: cat products, dog toys, home-based consumer products, and so on.

Seven-Step Strategic Planning Process

1. Brainstorm by asking questions
2. Generate answers or solutions (identify who came up with the idea)
3. Identify categories for ideas
4. Assign a team leader to each category
5. Prioritize the categories by value to the company
6. Assign each idea to a category
7. Prioritize ideas within a category

Repeat this Seven-Step Strategic Planning Process for each time frame. Due to the time that may be required to work through each time frame, you may need to limit this to one or two time frames. For example: time frame 1 = now to five years; time frame 2 = greater than five years. Feel free to adjust the time frame intervals as best suits your specific needs.

Action Plan

Once the team has developed groups of opportunities organized into two or three time frames, the team will need to develop an action plan to translate these results into specific products, product enhancements, or new market opportunities. Team leaders will need to be assigned to each category to facilitate further refinement of the ideas the team decides to develop further. Each team leader for a particular group of ideas will be the champion for those ideas and will help to communicate the ideas to the larger group or to the management team.

Before completing these strategic planning sessions, which may span over a few days, the facilitators should have team leaders who were assigned to each category pull together a small team. The small team should consist of the individual who generated the idea along with other appropriate thinkers to develop the details associated with the top ideas in their assigned category. This can be done using break-out sessions during the meeting, if there is time allocated, or it can be done by the assigned teams following the strategic planning session. In either case, a follow-up session should be planned to go over the results for the benefit of the entire group that participates.

For those highly energized teams with time to work on this effort, there is no restriction on the number of ideas to develop further in each category. However, most companies and teams have existing deadlines and other ongoing concerns, so that facilitators will have to set reasonable expectations. I recommend focusing on the top three to six ideas in each idea category. A good tool to use for this process is the Invention Disclosure Form presented earlier in this book. Have the team provide as much detail as possible and include diagrams (even rough sketches) to further develop the idea. The more detail they are able to develop, the better.

The facilitators should meet with each team leader and their team that was assembled to work on a particular category to discuss the ideas and ask questions. Once the facilitators and the team leader agree that the team has developed the detail necessary in the Invention Disclosure

Forms, the forms can be sent to a patent professional to start the patent application process.

Patent Professional Support

It is important to remember that each Invention Disclosure Form you send to a patent professional will result in the expense associated with the development of a patent application. For example, if your company has ten Invention Disclosure Forms, you will need to allocate the resources necessary to develop ten patent applications. This will not only take time from the team members and management team, it could also result in patent professional and related expenses north of $100,000 (as an example wherein each application is projected to cost approximately $10,000).

You will also want your executive management team or a group of team leaders participating in a committee (which could be named the patent review committee) to review the ideas. If there is a patent review committee assigned to review the ideas and identify those ideas they wish to pursue, they should also spend time assessing the prior art to get a sense of the probability of receiving a patent for the idea.

If your company does not have the expertise or resources to have a patent review committee, your executive management team will need to pick out the ideas they want to send to the patent professional based on the executive team's knowledge of the market and their available resources.

The Innovation Summit

Most companies have off-site meetings where a team is assembled and the team talks about ideas outside of the context of their normal daily duties, as described above in the brainstorming section. Let's run through an example of what a team might do if they were to have an off-site meeting specifically dedicated to innovation. Let's call the meeting the "innovation summit" and establish a time frame from one to three days for it. *Note that the meeting can go as long as you desire; however, after a couple days, your team members may start to get distracted as their "real jobs," which were put on the back burner, start to boil over!*

Before we simply grab a team of people and tell them to have an innovation summit and innovate, we need to think about the information and process you will use for your particular business situation. The goal of creating an innovation summit is to create a repeatable process that can be used periodically for the development of new ideas. Most importantly, the team will also need to feel it is a good use of their time.

Innovation Summit Checklist

An innovation summit checklist will be helpful to properly plan the innovation summit meeting.

- **Selecting the team members**

Select a team of individuals from all parts of the company. For a team of individual inventors, include inventors from different disciplines. A cross-functional team will provide a wide range of ideas and perspectives that will be helpful during the process. Remember, it doesn't matter where good ideas from. You may get your best ideas from the file clerk!

- **Putting together a list of questions**

The executive management team or assigned project leader should work with the facilitator prior to the session to generate questions that will be most appropriate for the team. Specific questions dealing with your specific business or situation will help the team to be more focused.

- **Analyzing possible answers**

These answers will help to establish problem statements that are most appropriate for the business. Having both questions and possible answers ahead of time will help to keep the session moving should the facilitator get the blank stare of a team wanting to check their e-mail.

- **Defining the problem statement**

The problem statement will help generate additional ideas as the team works to solve the problem. The process of generating answers to the questions established prior to the meeting and the formation of problem statements can be done in real-time with the team. However, I recommend that the facilitator work with the project leader or executive management team to establish enough material before meeting with the team in order to prime the pump with the team and get them started. As shown earlier in the book, examples are extremely important to convey your message.

- **Organizing the agenda**

Your agenda should be circulated to the team members prior to the meeting and should include the prework material you established. That is, you should include questions, possible answers, and example problem statements. Providing this material ahead of time to each team member will get him or her thinking prior to the meeting and talking with each other.

- **Starting the meeting**

You will want to establish the ground rules for those participating. You will need to set expectations that everyone will participate. Then review the agenda and answer any questions that come up. It may also be helpful to provide some background about the earlier concepts presented in this book regarding asking questions, analyzing the answers, and forming the problem statement. This will help the team understand what was done to establish the problem statements with which you will start the meeting.

For companies, I've found it is very helpful to have a senior executive speak at the beginning of the meeting to stress to the team how important the innovation summit meeting is to the company. This will reinforce to the team that it is worth their time.

- **Managing meeting dynamics**

Besides the traditional topics of interest associated with meeting dynamics, the one behavior you will want to manage is when team members describe solutions they have recently sold or offered for sale or short-term solutions that are being deployed already.

You will want to remind the team that if their ideas do move forward as patent applications, it will take a few years to get the USPTO to evaluate them. Additionally, if the patent application results in an issued patent, the patent will be enforceable for twenty years. Thus press the team to think of the big picture and only occasionally jump down into the weeds to validate an idea or suggestion. You will need to encourage and remind people that there are no bad ideas during the meeting. Reiterate to the team to focus on ideas and solutions, not on shooting down or debating the value of ideas.

It is essential to establish a safe environment in which questions may be asked and ideas communicated without fear of criticism or retribution. So often, great ideas remain between the ears of prospective inventors concerned with how they may be perceived.

- **Capturing the ideas**

As with traditional brainstorming techniques, the ideas can be written on individual slips of paper and tacked on the walls around the room, or the ideas can be written on an easel. When a page is full, it can be placed on the wall around the perimeter of the room. The most important point to remember is to surround the team with all of their ideas and solutions during the meeting, as they may shift their attention from the facilitator to an idea that was previously discussed and want to add more details to it or change it.

- **Categorizing the ideas**

This is where the team will identify category themes for groups of ideas and start to group their ideas into particular categories. These categories will need to be prioritized as related to business importance, which may be done within the meeting or as a follow-on meeting.

- **Assigning team leaders**

The facilitator will then work with the group to assign a team leader to each category (for small groups, there may be only one team leader). Each team leader will facilitate the following either in a break-out session or as a follow-on meeting:

- Prioritize ideas within a category
- Identify prior art for the top ideas in each category
- Fill out the Invention Disclosure Form

For those companies that wish to minimize the impact to the development staff, the idea priority step can also be accomplished with a small group of team leaders, managers, or executives to identify which of the ideas are worth developing further as patent applications.

- **Follow-up meeting**

A follow-up meeting should be scheduled and milestones identified for the teams to ensure everyone stays on track with this effort once they get back to their normal routines. This is one of the most challenging aspects of the effort, as many of the team members will be pulled in many different directions after the meeting. It is critical to ensure executive management supports the effort and considers it a priority for the company.

Examples of Possible Idea Categories

As discussed earlier, categories are identifiers that represent the theme for a group of ideas that is meaningful to the team. Some possible examples of categories for technical-related groups of ideas could include the following:

- Core infrastructure
- User interfaces
- Applications
- Services
- Communications
- Networks
- Hardware devices
- Application server providers
- Servers
- Clients
- Systems
- Databases
- Wireless applications

Oftentimes, it is helpful to divide the categories into subcategories that are simply just a refinement of the main category theme into related groupings. Using categories with subcategories will allow the team to assign a team leader to the main category, which would include all the subcategories as well.

For example, the following is a single category example with multiple subcategories where sample ideas have been grouped to give you an idea how this would work. These sample ideas are also prioritized:

Category: Applications

Subcategory: Reporting

1. Eliminate columns to make more readable
2. Provide subtotals on every other page
3. Optimize the processing of reporting data
4. Cache information for commonly generated reports

Subcategory: Credit Card Processing

1. Create a link between customers
2. Route direct to processing center
3. Avoid database access

Subcategory: Debit Card Processing

1. Automatically select between credit card and debit card
2. Expedite pin processing
3. Increase limits
4. Add security improvements

Subcategory: Affinity Program

1. Offer better rewards
2. Allow the use of frequent flyer miles
3. Allow the purchase of points
4. If customer has more than one million points, send free offers

Subcategory: Mailer

1. Automatically send mail when this special event occurs
2. Improve printing system to save time
3. Use the Internet

Alternatively, the team may decide that there is no need for subcategories and just identify these as categories. For example:

Category: Reporting Applications

1. Eliminate columns to make more readable
2. Provide subtotals on every other page
3. Optimize the processing of reporting data
4. Cache information for commonly generated reports

Category: Credit Card Processing Applications

1. Create a link between customers
2. Route direct to processing center
3. Avoid database access

Category: Debit Card Processing Applications

1. Automatically select between credit card and debit card
2. Expedite pin processing
3. Increase limits
4. Add security improvements

Category: Affinity Program Applications

1. Offer better rewards
2. Allow the use of frequent flyer miles
3. Allow the purchase of points
4. If customer has more than one million points, send free offers

Category: Mailer Applications

1. Automatically send mail when this special event occurs
2. Improve printing system to save time
3. Use the Internet

Some of these ideas will simply be product enhancements, also described as new product features, while others may have potential and be worth developing into patent applications. This is where the team leader assigned to the category will need to scrub the list with the team members who were assigned to the category in order to identify unique ideas worth exploring further for patent protection versus ideas that are simply product improvements. Not all of the ideas your team comes up with will be novel enough to patent, but many of these ideas may be excellent enhancements to your existing products.

Some ideas may be tagged as "product features," for those ideas that will enhance a product without becoming a patent application, and others as "possible patents," for those ideas that the team may wish to identify as candidates for a patent application.

Category: Applications
(Possible patentable ideas below are in bold)
Subcategory: Reporting

1. Eliminate columns to make more readable—product feature
2. Provide subtotals on every other page—product feature
3. **Optimize the processing of reporting data—possible patent**
4. Cache information for commonly generated reports—product feature

Subcategory: Credit Card Processing

1. Create a link between customers—product feature
2. Route direct to processing center—product feature
3. Avoid database access—product feature

Subcategory: Debit Card Processing

1. Automatically select between credit card and debit card—product feature
2. **Expedite pin processing in a unique way—possible patent**
3. Increase limits—product feature
4. **Add unique security improvements—possible patent**

Subcategory: Affinity Program

1. **Offer better rewards using new server design—possible patent**
2. Allow the use of frequent flyer miles—product feature

3. **Allow the purchase of points using new server design—possible patent**
4. **If customer has more than one million points, send free offers—possible patent**

Subcategory: Mailer

1. **Automatically send mail when this special event occurs—possible patent**
2. Improve printing system to save time—product feature
3. **Use the Internet in unique way—possible patent**

Example: Sample Ideas—Invention Disclosure Form

From the example above, here is the list of category/subcategory ideas identifying only the applicable bullets that need to be developed further into patent applications using the Invention Disclosure Form. Priorities may be assigned to these ideas based on your overall budget, which may be different from the original list of priorities above:

Possible Patent Opportunities from the Innovation Summit
Category: Applications
Subcategory: Reporting

- **Optimize the processing of reporting data—possible patent**

Subcategory: Debit Card Processing

- **Expedite pin processing in a unique way—possible patent**
- **Add unique security improvements—possible patent**

Subcategory: Affinity Program

- **Offer better rewards using new server design—possible patent**
- **Allow the purchase of points using new server design—possible patent**
- **If customer has more than one million points, send free offers—possible patent**

Subcategory: Mailer

- **Automatically send mail when this special event occurs—possible patent**
- **Use the Internet in unique way—possible patent**

Example: Sample Ideas—Product Enhancement List

From the original example above, here is the list of category/subcategory ideas identifying only the applicable bullets that will be assigned to the development teams as product features to be included within their product enhancement list. These won't be turned into patent applications, but the ideas are useful to include as new functionality for existing products that may have a positive impact on the popularity of the product with customers.

It is important to note that even though these ideas were not necessarily novel, they are still useful:

<u>Possible Product Enhancement Opportunities from the Innovation Summit</u>

Category: Applications

Subcategory: Reporting

- Eliminate columns to make more readable—product feature
- Provide subtotals on every other page—product feature
- Cache information for commonly generated reports—product feature

Subcategory: Credit Card Processing

- Create a link between customers—product feature
- Route direct to processing center—product feature
- Avoid database access—product feature

Subcategory: Debit Card Processing

- Automatically select between credit card and debit card—product feature
- Increase limits—product feature

Subcategory: Affinity Program

- Allow the use of frequent flyer miles—product feature

Subcategory: Mailer

- Improve printing system to save time—product feature

The examples shown in this chapter were used only to help provide perspective and are not the only methods for grouping ideas. The objective is simply for you to craft and shape the team's ideas as best fits your company's objectives to have the most impact for your particular project.

Five Points to Remember for the Facilitator

Here are five useful points to remember for conducting an innovation summit.

1. Set expectations
2. Communicate clearly
3. Use many examples
4. Involve all participants
5. Provide positive feedback to reward participation

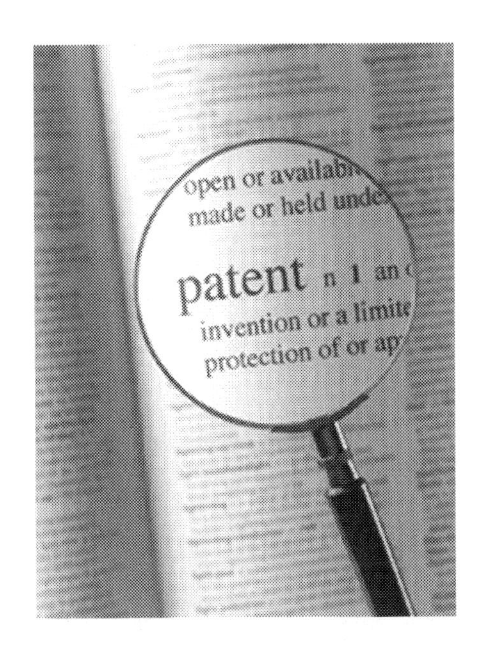

Chapter 6: Ready, Set, Go: The Patent Application

So many innovations have made our lives better. Here are just a few of them:

- Personal computer
- Cell phone
- Compact disc
- Vacuum cleaner
- Transistor
- Ballpoint pen
- Zipper
- Hair dryer
- Windshield wiper
- Coffee maker

- Automobile
- Airplane
- Light bulb
- Steam engine
- Telegraph
- Telephone
- Television
- Barbed wire
- Sewing machine
- MRI
- GPS
- Microscope
- Genetic sequencing
- Microwave

Many of these innovations have received patents or have patents associated with specific parts of them. Their inventors decided to act on their ideas, and some not only developed a new product but also took the time to apply for a patent on their ideas.

So let's see why you would want to apply for a patent on your ideas and how this could work for you.

A Few Good Reasons

First, why would you want to apply for a patent? Well, a few good reasons include the following:

- You may want to protect your invention and block others by filing a patent application, thereby establishing prior art so others cannot receive a patent on your invention. (Note that the first to invent is the one who is entitled to a patent in the United States, but it is also important to have some kind of documented proof that you were indeed the first to invent.)
- If you are issued a patent on your invention, you receive legally enforceable rights to prevent others from selling products incorporating your invention.

- You may want to build a strategic patent portfolio to add value to your company by creating intellectual property assets covering your novel products and novel product features in the form of patents.
- If you are issued a patent on your invention, you may wish to license the rights to practice your invention to others and receive royalties.
- Of course, there are many other reasons to obtain a patent; depending on your personal goals or business objectives, they should be discussed with your patent professional. Based on my experience, it can be an expensive process depending on the detail and technology associated with the patent application and can range anywhere from $5,000 and up per patent application. But the potential financial upside if you receive a patent and are able to license it to a company or use the patent to add value to your own business can be well worth the time and expense.

Justifying the Cost

Now, let's say you are convinced you want to try and get a patent on your ideas and decide to spend the time and money necessary to have a patent application written and filed on those ideas. You need to feel confident that the time and expense will be worth it to you. In other words, if it costs you $7,000 to file your patent application, can you expect at least $7,000 or more in revenue related to it?

As I have demonstrated through my personal experience, there are no guarantees that your issued patent will generate revenue. So I have found the best approach for me has been to develop plans to market and sell my ideas, such as the pet toy or self-watering plant container inventions described earlier.

I ask my patent professional for an estimate of costs and build business plans around the specific invention to get a clear picture on the overall costs and revenue prospects *before* I start spending money.

I then file a patent application when the invention is critical to the success of my new business venture and to further protect my idea, but only after feeling confident about the overall accounting projections and my prospects for a positive return on investment.

This requires me to do research on the prospects of marketing and selling my invention and more research on the novelty of my invention. It is extremely important to sort these details out *before* you start spending money on filing patent applications.

You must be careful not to let your excitement and passion for your idea overshadow the reality of realistic revenue potential and the likelihood that your idea will result in a patent being issued.

If you file a patent application in the hopes that you can sell the patent application or license it to a company, be prepared to spend a great deal of time researching the likelihood of interested companies, the market prospects of your invention, and whether these prospective companies have licensed patents from individual inventors. From experience, I know this route is *extremely* difficult, although I was successful in licensing the pet toy patents described earlier.

If you need to receive venture capital before you will be able to proceed with producing your idea, most venture capitalists will ask you if you have a patent or patent application filed on your idea. Why do they ask? These venture capitalists ask simply to get a sense of the uniqueness of your idea and your ability to fend off competition. Also note that filing a patent application on your ideas prior to discussions with third parties, such as venture capitalists, clearly establishes that you were the one who conceived the ideas (assuming, of course, there is no existing prior art).

From experience, I also recommend talking to your patent attorney before discussing pending patent applications with prospective investors or companies, as there may be legal implications to consider.

Starting the Process

To start the patent application process, you will need to have a patent professional help you write a patent application on your invention. Remember, it could take years to go through the evaluation and approval process with United States Patent and Trademark Office. There is even a chance that you may never receive a patent on your idea if prior art (we will discuss prior art in an upcoming chapter) is found that predates your invention. But let's say that after the evaluation process, the USPTO does allow your invention to become a U.S. patent; what does that mean?

Generally, the best way to think about what it means to receive a patent on your invention is that you receive the exclusive right from the U.S. government to your invention, specifically defined by your claims, for a certain period of time. This means the claims in your patent will define the scope and coverage of your patent as it relates to your invention.

The U.S. government gives you this exclusive right to your invention in exchange for your detailed, public disclosure of the invention. In other words, after your exclusivity period ends, your invention goes into the public domain for anyone to make, use, or sell.

A side note: If you do not want to publicly disclose your invention, you may want to treat it as a trade secret[11] or confidential information by simply keeping it secret and hoping no one ever comes up with the same thing. An example of a trade secret might be some fantastic method and fertilization formula for making plants grow that you developed. You may wish to keep this method and formula secret. In that case, you would *not* apply for a patent on it. Another well-known example of a trade secret is the Coca-Cola Company's famous formula for Coca-Cola®.[12]

Obtaining a Patent

There are many requirements and details associated with obtaining a patent on your invention, including the following:

- Your patent application must be "enabling," in other words defined well enough for someone of ordinary skill in the art to practice the invention from the information disclosed in your patent application.
- You must disclose the "best mode" in your patent application. Generally, this means you must disclose your

11 Trade secret described in more detail: www.wipo.int/sme/en/ip_business/trade_secrets/trade_secrets.htm,

12 Coca-Cola is a registered trademark of The Coca-Cola Company.

- entire invention and disclose the preferred embodiments or versions of your invention.
- The downside previously mentioned is after the allowed exclusivity period is over, your invention goes into the public domain for anyone to make, use, or sell.

Another way to think of a patent, once allowed by the USPTO, is as intellectual property rights analogous to owning a plot of land for a specific time frame. The land you own is defined by the location. Oftentimes, you will place a fence around your land to distinguish it from the land of others around you.

In the case of a patent, the fence around your intellectual property is defined by the claims in your patent that are allowed by the USPTO. The USPTO gives an inventor a certain amount of time for this exclusivity. There are different exclusivity time periods depending on your specific scenario and the type of patent you obtain, but generally you can think of this time period for the type of patent examples (utility patents) used in this book to be twenty years from the earliest filing date of the patent application.

But remember, the exclusivity is specifically related to that which is claimed and allowed by the USPTO in the patent section known as the claims, which will be described later in this chapter.

Much of the patent application format is very detailed and difficult to read. This is in part due to the USPTO rules and regulations, but is also due to the history of patent cases decided by the courts.

U.S. Patent Types

There are three basic U.S. patent types to be aware of: utility patents, design patents, and plant patents. Definitions of these U.S. patent types are as follows:

- **Utility Patent:** "*A utility patent covers the subject matter of the article used and how it works*" (35 U.S.C. 101). The examples within this book, including the pet toy and zucchini inventions, are all utility patents and utility patent applications.

- **Design Patent:** In section 1502 of the USPTO's *Manual of Patent Examining Procedure*, the definition of a design patent is as follows: *"In a design patent application, the subject matter which is claimed is the design embodied in or applied to an article of manufacture (or portion thereof) and not the article itself."* In other words, this type of U.S. patent covers the ornamental design or, in other words, how a design "looks."
- **Plant Patent:** "*Whoever invents or discovers and asexually reproduces any distinct and new variety of plant, including cultivated sports, mutants, hybrids, and newly found seedlings, other than a tuber propagated plant or a plant found in an uncultivated state, may obtain a patent*" (35 U.S.C. 16).

This type of U.S. patent (plant patent) will not be of interest to most inventors reading this book, unless you are working on creating something like a palm tree combined with a giant rose bush. Now, that would be very cool! Perhaps my next project (and the subject matter for the next book in this series) will be "The Rose Palm Tree." ☺

Provisional Patent Application

Another option to be discussed further with your patent professional is the option of initially filing a provisional patent application rather than a nonprovisional patent application.

Generally speaking, a provisional patent application enables you to spend less money up front to get your invention on file with the USPTO. It essentially establishes a filing date with the USPTO and enables you to refer to your invention as "Patent Pending." But you will still need to eventually (within one year) file a nonprovisional patent application. Thus you will essentially be spending more money in the long run.

Also remember that if you cut corners on the detailed description of your provisional patent application to save money, any new material detail you add later when you file the nonprovisional patent application will get a *new* filing date. So filing a provisional patent application really only saves you costs related to adding in claims and some filing fees.

Why would you want to file a provisional patent application? Well, here are some common reasons:

- If you have limited funds now and want to establish your filing date before you begin talking to prospective companies that may want to license your invention in hopes of obtaining additional funding.
- If you are in a rush and need to get a patent application on file with the USPTO for any number of time-to-market reasons.
- Maybe you are not sure about how your invention should be placed within the market or need more market information before you can write the claims for your invention.
- Perhaps you want to present your invention to a customer or at a trade show but want to get a filing date prior to that presentation.

There are other possible reasons that will depend on your particular situation. The key point here is that going this route is a less-expensive way to start the process and officially get your invention on file with the USPTO.

There are some downsides to this approach. One of the downsides is simply the fact that in order to receive a filing date for your provisional patent application, you still need to properly disclose your invention in the required detail and include any drawings required to describe your invention. Therefore, the only section you really can leave out are the claims, which can wait until you file your nonprovisional patent application on this same invention.

Additionally, any evaluation of your patent application by the USPTO will wait until you file the nonprovisional patent application. In other words, the USPTO will not even look at your provisional patent application until you file the nonprovisional patent application.

I know this option sounds confusing and I suppose that is why many patent professionals just recommend jumping into the swimming pool and spending the time and money to get a nonprovisional patent application on file with the USPTO. So discuss this with your patent professional and decide which route is best for you based on your situation. The bottom line related to a provisional patent application is that you still need to disclose all the detail about your invention as we have previously described in this chapter, but you do get to leave out the claims.

A final note on this topic: The provisional patent application option does not apply to design patent applications. But for all the inventions described in this book (i.e., utility patent applications and patents), filing a provisional patent application would have been an option.

Dissecting the Patent Application

It is extremely important that you as an inventor, team leader, or team member know what to expect from the patent professional, who may ask you questions throughout the process. So the U.S. nonprovisional patent application publication example that follows should be considered core information that you can use to be more informed when you interact with the patent professional you hire.

Being an informed and educated client will make the experience with the patent professional much more pleasant and cost effective, and will ensure that your invention is covered by the written patent application and that it claims what you expect it to claim.

Note that if the claims within this patent application are allowed by the USPTO, the patent application publication will convert to an issued U.S. patent. The format of the U.S. patent is the same as the U.S. patent application publication except for a few minor differences, such as the inclusion of references cited and a number change from a patent application publication number to a U.S. patent number, along with the date when the U.S. patent was issued. As such, the example that follows will focus on key areas of interest using a U.S. patent application publication.

The Patent Application Publication Format

The patent application itself consists of a number of key subject and information areas. This is very important to understand, as you will be required to review your application once the patent professional has completed drafting it. Your patent professional may also ask you to review a few patent applications and patents that showed up during a prior art search or showed up as part of an Office Action related to your application by a USPTO patent examiner.

Fear not; rejection of your application by the USPTO doesn't always mean that great idea of yours, which required you to spend so much time and money, is going into the trash bin.

This is the part of the process with the USPTO where your patent professional will articulate why the USPTO patent examiner's rejection is improper and why your claims are novel and different from the patent publications the USPTO examiner may reference. This is called patent prosecution and is one of the key reasons why you will need to pay a professional to ensure that you receive the protection you desire for your invention.

But don't be alarmed; your patent professional will not expect you to know the rules and regulations of the USPTO. However, he or she will ask you to review the similarities and differences between your invention and the publications he or she sends to you to review.

From a practical perspective, knowing what technology exists in the field of your invention helps you as an inventor. We will discuss in an upcoming chapter the definition of prior art and why you need to disclose anything of relevance regarding the prior art you know about to the USPTO. You will have a chance to clearly articulate the differences between your patent application and what already exists, which is also known as prior art. Your patent professional will emphasize the details of your invention that are novel (new and never been done before) within your patent application.

Oftentimes, knowing more about the prior art may even give you additional new ideas that you may wish to include when describing the details of your invention.

To help explain the format of the patent application publication, the previous example on the tissue package mirror will be described and broken down into sections that will be referenced by number.

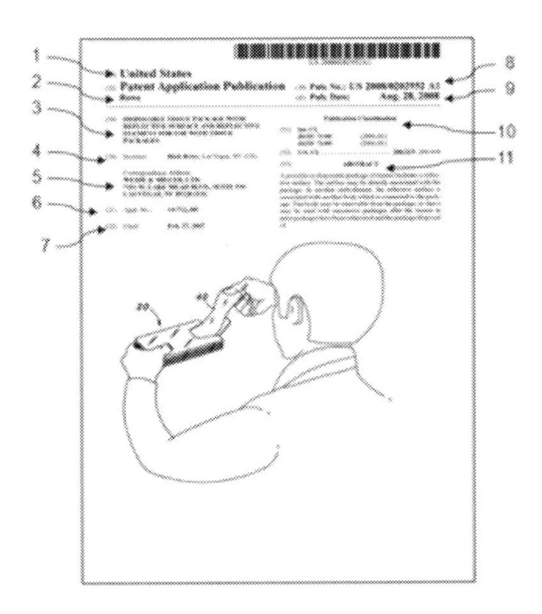

The Cover Page

Patent Application Publication Breakdown

The key subject and information areas of the patent and patent application consist of the following:

- **Cover Page Information Sections**
- **Abstract**
- **Field of Invention**
- **Background**
- **Summary**
- **Description of the Drawings**
- **Drawings**
- **Detailed Description of the Invention**
- **Claims**

Cover Page Information Sections

As illustrated in the cover page figure representing the patent application publication above, key information areas include the following:

United States Patent Application Publication (Section 1): "Patent application" means this application has *not* been issued as a U.S. patent, but is instead a patent application that has been published by the USPTO. Once you submit a patent application, it will generally take eighteen months before your nonprovisional patent application gets published. Once it is published, the public will be able to see your patent application and follow the interaction your patent professional has with the USPTO regarding your patent application.

Publication Number (Section 8): This is the unique number assigned to the patent application by the USPTO: **US 2008/0202952 A1.**

Publication Date (Section 9): This is the date on which the patent application was published by the USPTO: **Aug 28, 2008.**

Title (Section 3): The title of the patent application provided by the patent professional: **Disposable tissue package with reflective surface and reflective element for use with tissue packages.**

Inventor (Sections 2 and 4): The name of the person identified as the inventor (this could include multiple names when there are multiple inventors): Rowe, Rick; **Las Vegas, NV, United States of America.**

Correspondence Address (Section 5): This information will include the name and address of the patent professional with whom the USPTO will interact during the prosecution process.

Application Number (Section 6): A unique number assigned to the patent application by the USPTO when it was initially filed: **11/712, 185.**

Filed (Section 7): The date when the application was filed: **Feb 27, 2007.**

Publication Classifications (Section 10): These are the classification numbers associated with your invention derived from the field of your invention (Section 12 on Page 2 of the patent application below). The USPTO will search these classifications for prior art.

Abstract

The ***Abstract*** **(Section 11)** is a very brief description of the overall invention:

A portable or disposable package of tissues includes a reflective surface. The surface may be directly associated with the package. In another embodiment, the reflective surface is associated with another body, which is connected to the package. That body may be removable from the package, so that it may be used with successive packages after the tissues in prior packages have been exhausted and the package disposed of.

The following page of the patent application publication will be referenced with the section numbers as shown:

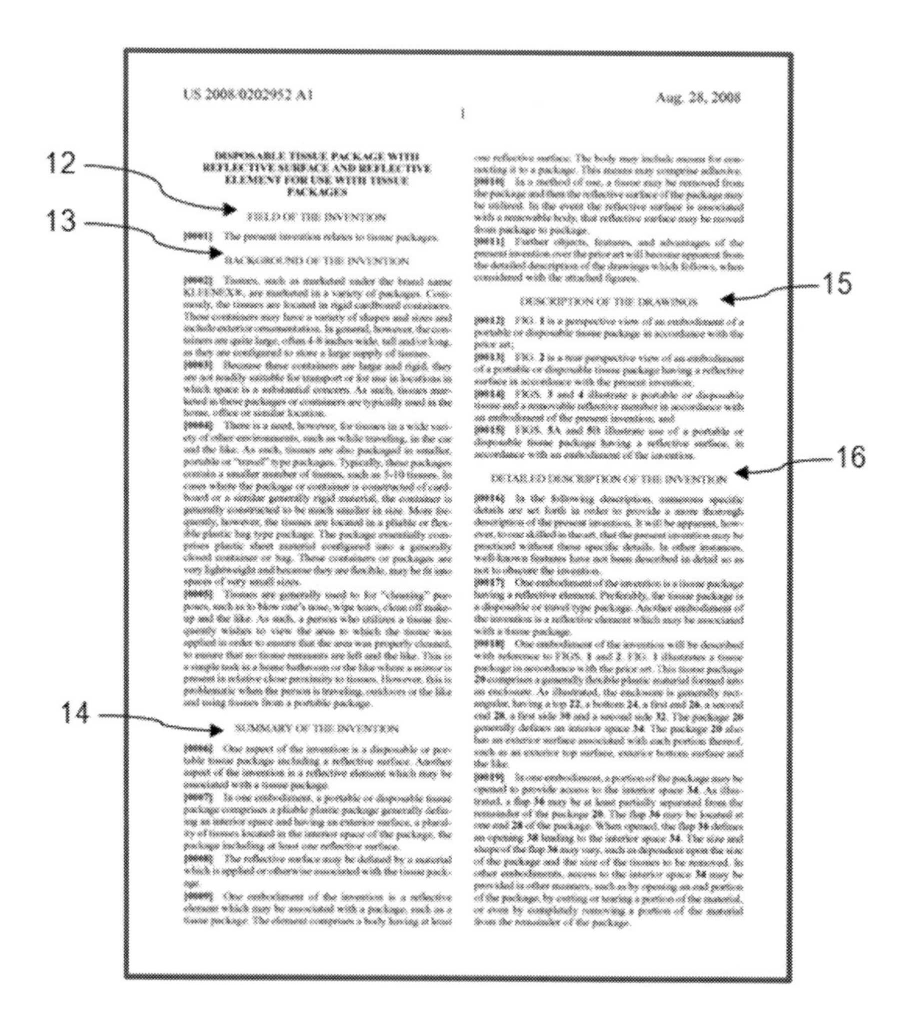

US 2008/0202952 A1 Aug. 28, 2008

1

DISPOSABLE TISSUE PACKAGE WITH REFLECTIVE SURFACE AND REFLECTIVE ELEMENT FOR USE WITH TISSUE PACKAGES

FIELD OF THE INVENTION

[0001] The present invention relates to tissue packages.

BACKGROUND OF THE INVENTION

SUMMARY OF THE INVENTION

DESCRIPTION OF THE DRAWINGS

DETAILED DESCRIPTION OF THE INVENTION

Field of Invention

The ***Field of Invention*** **(Section 12)** articulates the area of art or technology where this invention fits and is helpful to the USPTO to identify the classification of art to be used by the USPTO in evaluating the invention:

FIELD OF THE INVENTION

The present invention relates to tissue packages.

Background

The ***Background*** **(Section 13)** is helpful to the patent examiner to establish the problems or challenges with the prior art your invention solves. However, it is not required and not always present.

BACKGROUND OF THE INVENTION

Tissues, such as marketed under the brand name Kleenex®,[13] *are marketed in a variety of packages. Commonly, the tissues are located in rigid cardboard containers. These containers may have a variety of shapes and sizes and include exterior ornamentation. In general, however, the containers are quite large, often four to eight inches wide, tall, and/or long, as they are configured to store a large supply of tissues.*

Because these containers are large and rigid, they are not readily suitable for transport or for use in locations in which space is a substantial concern. As such, tissues marketed in these packages or containers are typically used in the home, office, or similar location.

There is a need, however, for tissues in a wide variety of other environments, such as while traveling, in the car, and the like. As such, tissues are also packaged in smaller, portable or "travel"-type packages. Typically, these packages contain a smaller number of tissues, such as five to ten tissues. In cases where the package or container is constructed of cardboard or a similar generally rigid material, the container is generally constructed to be much smaller in size. More frequently, however, the tissues are located in a pliable or flexible plastic bag-type package. The package essentially comprises plastic sheet material configured into a generally closed container or bag. These containers or packages are very lightweight and because they are flexible, may be fit into spaces of very small sizes.

Tissues are generally used to for "cleaning" purposes, such as to blow one's nose, wipe tears, clean off make-up, and the like. As such, a person who utilizes a tissue frequently wishes to view the area to which the tissue was applied in order to ensure that the area was properly cleaned, to ensure

13 Kleenex is a registered trademark of Kimberly-Clark Worldwide, Inc.

that no tissue remnants are left, and the like. This is a simple task in a home bathroom or the like where a mirror is present in relative close proximity to tissues. However, this is problematic when the person is traveling, outdoors, or the like and using tissues from a portable package.

Summary

The ***Summary*** **(Section 14)** provides the patent examiner with a summary of the invention in more detail than the ***Abstract*** **(Section 11)**, but not as detailed as the ***Detailed Description*** **(Section 16)**.

SUMMARY OF THE INVENTION

One aspect of the invention is a disposable or portable tissue package including a reflective surface. Another aspect of the invention is a reflective element, which may be associated with a tissue package.

In one embodiment, a portable or disposable tissue package comprises a pliable plastic package generally defining an interior space and having an exterior surface, a plurality of tissues located in the interior space of the package, the package including at least one reflective surface.

The reflective surface may be defined by a material that is applied or otherwise associated with the tissue package.

One embodiment of the invention is a reflective element, which may be associated with a package, such as a tissue package. The element comprises a body having at least one reflective surface. The body may include means for connecting it to a package. This means may comprise adhesive.

In a method of use, a tissue may be removed from the package and then the reflective surface of the package may be utilized. In the event the reflective surface is associated with a removable body, that reflective surface may be moved from package to package.

Further objects, features, and advantages of the present invention over the prior art will become apparent from the detailed description of the drawings, which follows, when considered with the attached figures.

Description of the Drawings

The ***Description of the Drawings*** **(Section 15)** identifies each drawing used by the ***Detailed Description*** **(Section 16)** of the patent application and provides a brief description of the drawing.

DESCRIPTION OF THE DRAWINGS

FIG 1 is a perspective view of an embodiment of a portable or disposable tissue package in accordance with the prior art;

FIG 2 is a rear perspective view of an embodiment of a portable or disposable tissue package having a reflective surface in accordance with the present invention;

FIG 3 and 4 illustrate a portable or disposable tissue and removable reflective member in accordance with an embodiment of the present invention; and

FIG 5A and 5B illustrate use of a portable or disposable tissue package having a reflective surface, in accordance with an embodiment of the invention.

Drawings

The drawings associated with the patent application as shown below usually span multiple pages depending on the number of drawings included to help describe the invention.

Figures 1 and 2

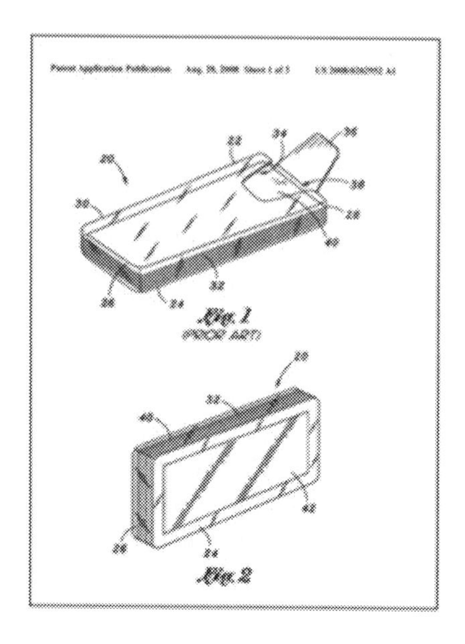

Figures 3 and 4

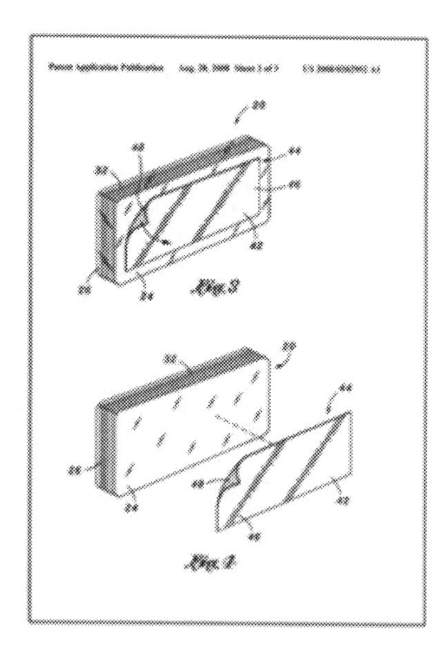

Figures 5A and 5B

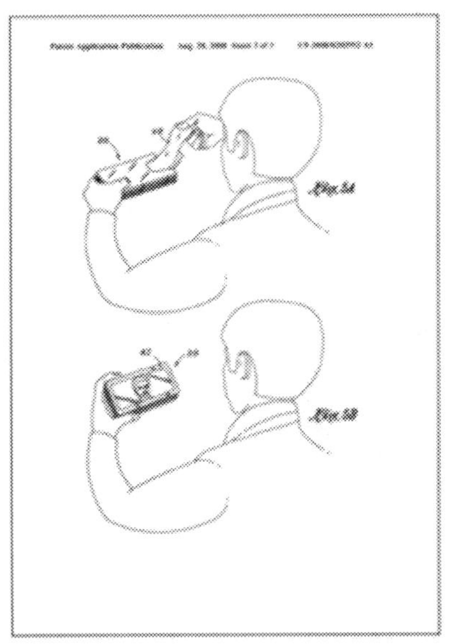

Detailed Description of the Invention

The **Detailed Description (Section 16)** of the patent application includes a detailed description of everything someone would need to know to build your invention. The written description is also called *constructive reduction to practice*. Note that within this section of the patent, a numbering system is used to associate the information described in the ***Detailed Description*** **(Section 16)** with a specific ***Figure*** or ***Drawing***. Each ***Figure*** is broken down into a series of reference numbers that can be identified by the reader of the patent application within the ***Detailed Description*** **(Section 16)**, as you will see below.

The detail presented in the patent/patent application publication is what makes patents so cool. The document itself becomes a teaching tool to teach the reader about the invention and how to build it. Next time you need to research a technology, just access www.google.com/Patents and enter a keyword or the name of the technology you are interested in. You will be presented with a list of patents and patent applications consisting of a large amount of information to read. Of course, when you read these publications, the legal language will cause some confusion for those not familiar with patent lingo.

Here are some examples of legal words you will come across in the publications with a general description you can use as a guideline:

- *Embodiment* (a concrete form of the idea)
- *Comprised of* (to be made up of, consisting at least of the following)
- *Said item* (previously used definition of item mentioned earlier in the patent application)

All these words have legal meanings. This is another reason why you are paying your patent professional to translate the information you provide into language that is understood by the USPTO and may ultimately be viewed by a judge and jury if litigation were to occur. Remember, your job is to *think* of those great ideas.

How does litigation work, you may ask? Well, one such example is when an inventor asserts an issued patent he or she owns against a company that is believed to be infringing their patent or practicing his or her invention. For example, if you owned a plot of land, you wouldn't want someone to pitch a tent on it without your permission, would you? So goes a patent. Once you have received your patent, you wouldn't want someone using your invention without permission or a license agreement.

These topics require the heavy lifting of a patent attorney (not a patent agent, as previously described) who understands all the appropriate details and who can provide the legal advice you need. We won't cover these topics in any more detail within this book. But one point to remember is that litigation can be a very costly endeavor, so make sure you spend time discussing the pros and cons of litigation with your patent attorney *before* you do anything threatening. That means *never* tell someone he or she is infringing your patent without talking to your attorney first! Let your patent attorney counsel you before you do or say anything inappropriate.

For those readers wanting more detail in how a patent application reads, actual patent application language is provided below. For others not interested in this detail, jump to the next section on ***Claims***.

Remember, as you work your way through the ***Detailed Description*** below (shown in Section 16), refer back to the drawings referenced by the figure number and associated item number within the ***Detailed Description*** text.

DETAILED DESCRIPTION OF THE INVENTION **(Section 16)**

In the following description, numerous specific details are set forth in order to provide a more thorough description of the present invention. It will be apparent, however, to one skilled in the art that the present invention may be practiced without these specific details. In other instances, well-known features have not been described in detail so as not to obscure the invention.

One embodiment of the invention is a tissue package having a reflective element. Preferably, the tissue package is a disposable or travel-type package. Another embodiment of the invention is a reflective element, which may be associated with a tissue package.

One embodiment of the invention will be described with reference to Figures 1 and 2. Figure 1 illustrates a tissue package in accordance with the prior art. This tissue package 20 comprises a generally flexible plastic material formed into an enclosure. As illustrated, the enclosure is generally rectangular, having a top 22, a bottom 24, a first end 26, a second end 28, a first side 30, and a second side 32. The package 20 generally defines an interior space 34. The package 20 also has an exterior surface associated with each portion thereof, such as an exterior top surface, exterior bottom surface, and the like.

In one embodiment, a portion of the package may be opened to provide access to the interior space 34. As illustrated, a flap 36 may be at least partially separated from the remainder of the package 20. The flap 36 may be located at one end 28 of the package. When opened, the flap 36 defines an opening 38 leading to the interior space 34. The size and shape of the flap 36 may vary, such as dependent upon the size of the package and the size of the tissues to be removed. In other embodiments, access to the interior space 34 may be provided in other manners, such as by opening an end portion of the package, by cutting or tearing a portion of the material, or even by completely removing a portion of the material from the remainder of the package.

One or more tissues 40 are located in the package. As illustrated, the tissues 40 may be folded into a configuration in which they match the cross-sectional shape of the package.

The material forming the package 20 may be generally transparent or clear. In this manner, the tissues 40 are visible through the package. This permits, for example, the user to determine the number of tissues remaining the package.

Referring to Figure 2, in accordance with one embodiment of the invention, the package 20 includes at least one reflective surface 42. In one embodiment, the reflective surface 42 comprises a reflective material which is associated with the package 20. For example, a metallic or other reflective material may be deposited on or into, adhered to, connected to, embedded in, or otherwise associated with the package 20. In one embodiment, as described in greater detail below, the reflective surface may be associated with another body or element which is itself associated with the package.

In one embodiment, as illustrated in Figure 2, the reflective surface 42 is located at the bottom 24 of the package 20. The reflective surface may be located at various areas or portions or the package 20, such as the top, sides, or the like (or combinations thereof). Preferably, the reflective surface 42 faces outwardly of the package 20. In one embodiment, the reflective surface 42 comprises a substantial portion of the surface area of the package 20, such as a substantial portion of the bottom 24 of the package 20, whereby the reflective surface 42 is sufficiently large to be utilized as a mirror.

In one embodiment, the reflective surface 42 is located at the exterior of the package 20. In another embodiment, the reflective surface 42 is simply visible from the exterior of the package 20. For example, if the package 20 is constructed from a transparent material, the reflective surface 42 might be located in or behind (i.e., at the interior of the package) that surface and thus still be visible to the user.

Another embodiment of the invention is illustrated in Figures 3 and 4. As illustrated therein, the reflective surface 42 is defined on or by a body 44 or member which is connected to the package 20. In a preferred embodiment, that body 44 is selectively connectable to the package 20. In one embodiment, the body 44 has a first side 46 and a second side

48. At least one of the sides defines the reflective surface 42. The other side is configured to be located adjacent to the package 20.

As one example, the body 44 might comprise a sheet of Mylar (a brand of DuPont) material having at least one reflective side. The body 44 might also comprise a substrate or base material which is non-reflective and which has a reflective material applied thereto on at least one side.

In one embodiment, means are provided for selectively connecting the body 44 to the package 20. This means might comprise adhesive, one or more fasteners, or the like. For example, an adhesive may be applied to the second side 48 of the body 44 for adhering the body 44 to the package 20.

A covering may be applied over the adhesive side of the body 44 before it is used. This covering may be peeled away to expose the adhesive the first time the body 44 is to be associated with a package 20.

In one embodiment, referring to Figures 3 and 4, the body 44 may be connected to a package 20 which does not otherwise include a reflective surface, thereby providing the package with a reflective surface. In addition, the body 44 may be removed from the package 20. For example, the body 44 might be removed from an empty package 20 before that package is thrown away. This may permit the body 44 to be associated with a different package. For example, the body 44 may then be associated with a new, full package 20.

In a preferred embodiment, the reflective surface (and a body with which it is associated, in such an embodiment) is pliable, permitting it to conform to changes in the shape of the package. For example, it is preferred that the reflective surface not prevent a flexible plastic or similar package such as that illustrated in Figure 1 from being folded or otherwise compressed into a different shape, as might occur if the package were being forced into a differently sized space (like a pocket or the like). In other embodiments, the reflective surface or member might be generally rigid, such as a reflective material applied to a plastic substrate.

Various aspects of the invention will now be appreciated. First, in accordance with the invention, a reflective surface is associated with a portable or disposable tissue package. In this manner, when the user uses a tissue, a reflective surface is conveniently provided for use by the user. For example, referring to Figure 5A, a user may remove a tissue 40 from the package 20 and then use that tissue. As illustrated in Figure 5B, the user may then turn the package over so that the reflective surface 42 faces them, so that they may see their face or another portion of their body.

In one embodiment, the reflective surface may be integral to the package. In this configuration, the reflective surface may be manufactured as an element of the package and be disposed with the package.

Another embodiment of the invention is a portable or removable reflective surface that may be associated with one or more packages. In this configuration, a user may obtain a reflective surface and associate it with a package. The user may also remove the reflective surface from one package and associate it with another package. For example, a consumer may purchase bulk package of four or six packages of tissues. A portable reflective surface may be associated with the bulk package or one of the individual packages and may be selectively connected to each of the individual packages as they are utilized.

In a preferred embodiment, the package with which the reflective element is associated is a pliable, plastic package. In other embodiments, however, the package might be of a variety of other configurations. For example, the tissue package might be constructed of paperboard or the like, and yet still be small in size so as to be portable/disposable.

The reflective surface may be used for a variety of purposes. For example, in the event of an emergency, the reflective surface might be used as a signaling device. In the case where the reflective surface is associated with a body which can be removed from the package, the body may be removed from the package and placed on another surface, such as the top of a car.

It will be understood that the above described arrangements of apparatus and the method there from are merely illustrative of applications of the principles of this invention and many other embodiments and modifications may be made without departing from the spirit and scope of the invention as defined in the claims.

Claims

Remember that the ***Claims*** **(Section 17)** define your property.

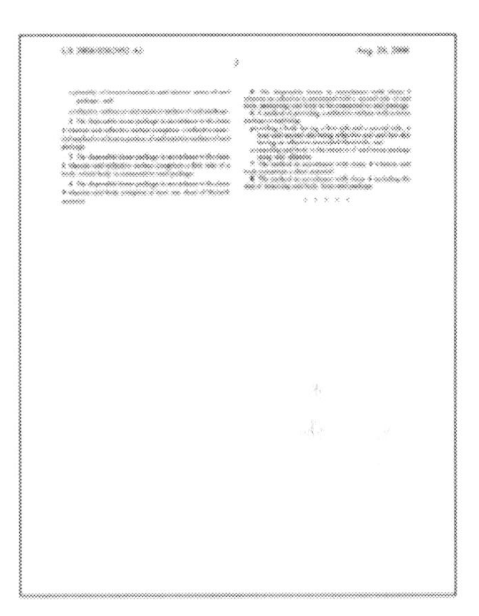

The ***Claims*** will be written by your patent professional and are especially important, so make sure your patent professional explains the claims he or she writes for your invention. In the ***Claims*** section of the patent, each word and arrangement of words has very special meaning for the patent coverage you may receive.

Also note that many times, inventors will read a patent and be extremely concerned by the written description. Just remember that the claims define the intellectual property and patent coverage so each word and element of the claim describes the exact coverage of the invention.

What is claimed is:

1. *A disposable tissue package comprising: a pliable plastic package generally defining an interior space and having an exterior surface; a plurality of tissues located in said interior space of said package; and a reflective surface at said exterior surface of said package.*

2. *The disposable tissue package in accordance with claim 1 wherein said reflective surface comprises a reflective material applied to at least a portion of said exterior surface of said package.*
3. *The disposable tissue package in accordance with claim 1 wherein said reflective surface comprises a first side of a body, which body is connected to said package.*
4. *The disposable tissue package in accordance with claim 3 wherein said body comprises at least one sheet of Mylar material.*
5. *The disposable tissue in accordance with claim 3 wherein an adhesive is associated with a second side of said body, permitting said body to be connected to said package.*
6. *A method of providing a reflective surface with a tissue package providing a body having a first side and a second side, at least said second side being reflective and said first side having an adhesive associated therewith; and connecting said body to the exterior of said tissue package using said adhesive.*
7. *The method in accordance with claim 6 wherein said body comprises a sheet material.*
8. *The method in accordance with claim 6 including the step of removing said body from said package.*

Chapter 7: That's Obvious, or Is It?

One topic that often does not get discussed between patent professionals and their clients, until later in the process, is the topic of obviousness. The USPTO can take a few years or longer before it starts to review your patent application. When the USPTO does start evaluating your patent application, the examiner assigned to evaluate your patent application may believe your invention, that idea you spent time and money creating, prototyping, and evolving, is obvious to someone with ordinary skill in the art; that is, someone who is knowledgeable in the technology and methodologies within the field in which your invention is intended.

Patent Prosecution

Patent prosecution is the process of your patent professional's interaction with the USPTO related to the evaluation and assessment of your patent application. This is when responses or actions will occur and when your invention may receive a rejection because of obviousness.

An obviousness rejection will be based on a patent, patent publication, or non-patent publication that the examiner has discovered in a prior art search that arguably describes your invention. The rejection will be sent to your patent professional, who will then contact you to discuss it. Most inventors I know have experienced the frustration of a patent rejection indicating that their invention is obvious in view of some combination of patent publications.

Obviousness Definition

So what is a good definition of *obviousness*?

Generally speaking, obviousness from a patent application perspective means that based on the claims of your invention, it would have been obvious to a person with ordinary skill in the art (in other words, skilled in your field of invention) to come up with the same thing you defined by your claims sometime before your date of conception.

This gets a little tricky; just remember that generally something is obvious if a person with ordinary skill in the art could have come up with the same solution based on the existing art in the field without any additional skill or ability.

Ultimately, the professional you hire will be the one to go head to head as your representative with the USPTO to argue why your invention is novel, not obvious, and why the references identified are different from your invention. This will cost you additional money, beyond what you spent for writing and filing your patent application.

You will be paying for your professional's time to interact with the USPTO as it relates to your patent application. This interaction will be to argue on your behalf that the claims of your patent application should be allowed as a patent.

This interaction is driven by Office Actions and has very important deadlines, so if your patent professional asks you questions or needs input in order to respond, get back to them quickly. Not responding in a timely manner will cost you additional money. Even worse, if you wait too long, your patent application will go abandoned.

So how can you avoid having your patent application rejected by the USPTO due to obviousness? Unfortunately, there is no way to guarantee that a reference or combination of references will not be found, prompting a rejection of your invention.

The USPTO will be evaluating your invention based on the field of your invention and the state of the art within the field of invention, so it will help to make sure your patent professional is properly prepared to argue that your invention in new, unique, novel, and *not* obvious. If you have done your research, you should be able to keep costs down and bolster the response to the USPTO.

For those thinking they can use a "do it yourself" patent service to file a patent application for you, I suggest contacting a patent professional instead. While you may be able to minimize up-front costs of filing a patent application, making sure that you have enough detail in your patent application and preparing for future Office Actions as previously described requires a patent professional. Taking shortcuts at the start of this process can cause you bigger issues later on, such as not having enough detail in your application to properly describe your invention.

To give you an example as to the length of time it takes for this process, the patent application for the **Disposable tissue package with reflective surface and reflective element for use with tissue packages** described earlier was filed in the beginning of 2007 and, as of the publication of this book (early 2010), is still going through the process.

Time, Money, and Research

A recent decision involving obviousness by the Supreme Court (KSR Int'l. Co. v. Teleflex Inc., No. 04-1350 April 30, 2007)[14] has made it more challenging to receive a U.S. patent. Basically, KSR argued that a combination of two elements related to specific technology involved in the lawsuit, for reasons described in the lawsuit, was obvious and should not be patentable, and the Supreme Court ruled in favor of KSR.

The detail of this particular legal case is far beyond the scope of this book; just remember that it is extremely important for you to do prior art searches and detailed research to insure the novelty of your invention to increase the likelihood that your patent application will produce a U.S. patent.

Over time, laws change and legal interpretations evolve as juries and courts rule on specific cases that influence patentability. So for those non-attorney readers (and writer) in the room, we just need to remember to focus on the details related to how and why our inventions are novel.

This simply means there is good reason for you to write down as much as possible and explain in detail why you believe your invention is

---

14 Interesting information on the topic: www.law.cornell.edu/supct/html/04-1350.ZS.html.

unique and worthy of a patent. Also be sure to include lots of diagrams, examples, and as many future features and configurations as you can dream up. Do your research!

No Guarantee

It is easy to get confused about what you can patent. Just remember that there are no guarantees that your invention described in your patent application will result in a patent. Yes, even after waiting years and spending thousands of dollars and many hours, you still may not receive a patent. I know that sounds pretty depressing, and most books I have read do not touch on this topic very well. So use the strategy of being an informed inventor as I have mentioned and include as much detail and information in your patent application as possible to help better your chances to obtain a patent.

But in my opinion, having a pending patent application on your invention is a much better alternative than not having one, since it clearly establishes you as the inventor and articulates your invention and how to build it in detail. Besides, your patent professional has done this before with many other inventors and uses a number of strategies to communicate the novelty of your invention to the USPTO.

So before you throw up your hands and decide to give up on spending the money to patent your idea, think again. There may be many reasons why your invention or aspects of your invention could receive patent protection.

Don't give up on your idea or invention until you have talked with your patent professional about the details. He or she will advise you based in part on all the research *you will provide him or her* regarding the possibility of obtaining a patent on your invention. He or she may even recommend additional steps you can take to further ensure that your invention is unique (novel), such as researching specific prior art he or she points out in the field of your invention.

If you ultimately decide not to work toward obtaining a patent on your invention after discussing it with a patent professional, your invention may still be a valuable product enhancement to an existing product (or even a new product). You may choose to focus specifically on introducing your innovative ideas to the marketplace as products with an objective of being first to market or being lower priced than your competitors. You will need to make these decisions based on your goals, objectives, and resources.

Helpful Rules of Thumb

- Ensure that your problem statement is clear and concise, and that the problem you are trying to solve is worth the investment you may decide to make.
- Make sure you add as many features and functions to your invention as you can dream up.
- Add new features, elements you create, elements that are unique to the field of the invention, create a new method, or solve the problem in a unique way.
- Do your research and be an expert in the field; know what has already been created and what products are already out in the field.
- Provide your patent professional with as much written detail as possible describing your idea, the state of the art, and why your invention is unique.

The bottom line is that there are no guarantees you will obtain a patent for your invention, so make sure you spend the time, effort, and money on those ideas you think are the most unique and worthwhile inventions to go through the patent application process.

Company-Related Efforts

Your company may have a legal department with the resources to do the prior art searches on the ideas your team develops. The legal department may even train your team on how to perform prior art searches. The key from my experience, as I have already discussed above, is to make sure your team does the product research and provides as much detail as possible on their inventions to the patent professional. Encourage your team to think of all those details and write them down using a template such as the Invention Disclosure Form described in this book. Developing a strong patent portfolio to cover the novel aspects of your products may help your company protect and defend their position in the marketplace.

Key Points to Remember

It is important to remember that you do not have an issued patent until the USPTO *allows* the claims in your patent application. This could take a number of years from the time you apply for the patent until you are ultimately awarded a patent, so take a breath once your patent professional submits your patent application to the USPTO. It will take a while to go through this entire patent process, so make sure your patent application includes how your invention will look in five years too; be creative and dream—add as many features and functions as you can dream up!

Once the USPTO does provide you with a Notice of Allowance, notifying you that the *claims* of your invention have been allowed, your patent application turns into an issued U.S. patent and is provided with a unique U.S. patent number.

Remember, there are situations, such as prior art showing up that you were unaware of, that may prevent you from receiving a patent on your invention. Doing your homework and making sure the prior art is different from your invention is extremely important in order to avoid the frustration of not receiving a patent later.

This is another important reason to make sure the detailed specification of your patent application includes all your ideas and all the possibilities you can think of relating to your invention. This will give your patent professional material to support different claims should it be necessary to modify the original claims.

You should make sure you define as many embodiments as you can dream up, so write down everything you can. Will this cost more? Sure it will. But this additional material will give your patent professional many options when crafting the claims of your invention and arguing the case of novelty with the USPTO.

Chapter 8: Prior Art, It Came Before

What is prior art, anyway? At a high level, prior art is simply all that has been done in the field of your invention and related fields before you conceived your invention. For example, if we had come up with an invention for a cat toy using a remote-controlled device (shown in the diagram below) in 2004 and filed a patent application on it in January of 2005, we should not celebrate yet.

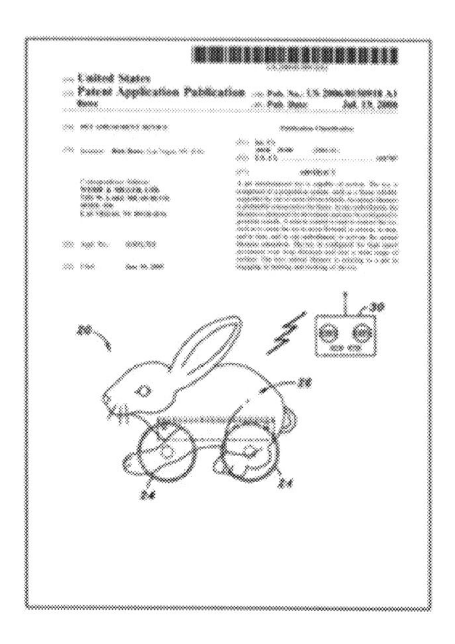

After the "The Patent Application" chapter, you now know the importance of your claims. Do the claims in your patent application cover technology that has already been described in an earlier publication or patent publication?

Let's say you looked around the marketplace and did not find any product offered that is the same as your invention and you start to feel pretty darned excited about your invention. Well, unfortunately, you're not out of the woods yet.

This is where the debate with the USPTO begins and where a bunch of rules and regulations come into play. For you as the inventor, you will have a patent professional to help you navigate these waters. But be aware that when your patent application is evaluated by the USPTO, they may find patent applications, patents, or publications that existed prior to the date you filed your patent application.

Going back to our example, further prior art searches revealed the following patent that was filed on June 10, 1996:

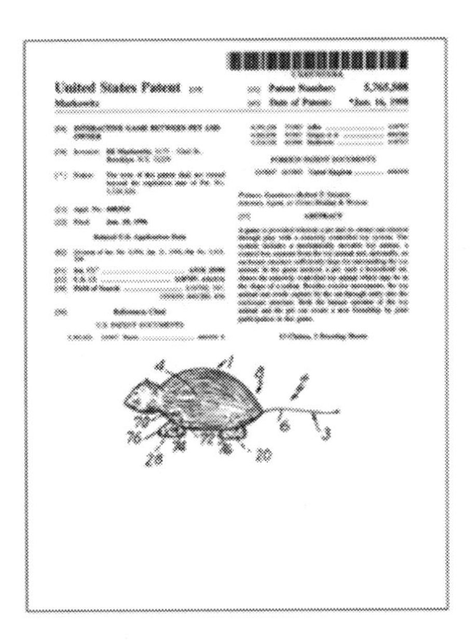
United States Patent

Now, we start to get a bit concerned, as this patent reads very close to the invention that we described in our patent application. It now comes down to the USPTO rules and regulations regarding prior art content and dates. Your patent professional will compare the content and claims of your patent application to the content (and claims, if applicable) of the patent application, patent, or publication cited by the USPTO.

In this example, the prior art patent that was cited has a filing date much earlier than our patent application filing date, and the content of the prior art patent actually describes our invention in detail. Thus we have a problem that we will probably not be able to overcome unless we can claim that there is something else in our patent application that is novel and not disclosed in the prior art patent.

Ultimately, we decided not to pursue the 2005 patent application we filed and instead purchased the 1996 patent directly from the individual inventor who owned the patent identified as prior art. This did cost us more money, but it was an alternative way of achieving our objectives of obtaining patent coverage on the technology we planned to sell.

Some of the solutions your patent professional will discuss with you when prior art rejections are made by the USPTO include changing the claims in your patent application to claims narrower than what you may have desired to claim, or canceling claims or amending claims to cover another aspect (embodiment) of the invention that was articulated in the patent application and not articulated in the prior art.

Another approach your patent professional may recommend is abandoning the pending patent application altogether and filing a continuation-in-part (CIP) patent application to add in new material that describes modifications to your invention to make it novel over the prior art. This will allow you to leverage the original filing date and all the material already written rather than starting over from scratch with a completely new application.

Continuation-In-Part Patent Applications

There is a catch with the CIP approach. Adding new material may help distinguish your invention from the prior art, but it has the side effect of establishing a *new* filing date for the new material that may cause new rejections to be raised by the USPTO examiner based on other prior art they may find.

That said, there are also benefits to filing a CIP. A CIP patent application can help you manage additional features you add to your invention after you have filed an application on your original idea. Such an approach may result in many new patent applications, as was described in the earlier pet toy example.

Oftentimes, these additional patent applications are referred to as child patent applications within a patent family that was started from a single patent application, known as the parent application, describing your original idea. This is because each of the child patent applications includes a reference to the parent patent application.

Prior Art Search

One way you can build more confidence that your invention *is not* obvious and *is* novel or unique is to pay your patent professional to perform prior art searches or hire a professional specializing in prior art searches.

This will cost you more money (possibly multiple hours, depending on the subject matter, at $150 to $350 per hour), but it is well worth it since the search results will be a list of patents and patent publications that may be similar to your invention. Reviewing the prior art collected during a prior art search will enable you to better define your invention to further distinguish it from the prior art that was found.

The patent professional will use keywords derived from the details of your invention and the field, and related fields, of your invention to perform the prior art search using patent databases and other sources. The collected information will then need to be reviewed and discussed. This information may also help inform the patent professional in order to make the appropriate modifications to your patent application before it is submitted to the USPTO.

Duty of Disclosure

Another important topic associated with prior art is the information disclosure that will be sent to the USPTO and associated with your patent application. It is important not to think you can keep something from the USPTO to ensure that you receive your patent. You, your representative, and anyone else associated with the development of the invention are required to disclose to the USPTO all publications, patent applications, and patents that you know of that may be applicable to your invention.

Typically, your patent professional will ask you for this information or ask you to fill out an Information Disclosure Statement (IDS). The IDS is simply a form that you will use to list the applicable information.

Disclosing to your patent professional early in the process what you know about the prior art along with who, what, and when related to your invention may save you thousands of dollars down the road. If you knew about a product that was for sale in the United States, a patent that was relevant to your invention, or a detailed product description in a publication that disclosed your invention that existed before you filed your patent application, and you decided not to disclose it, it could come back to haunt you later.

For example, let's say you actually receive a U.S. patent on your invention but you knew about a product in the United States that had been introduced and sold a few years earlier than the filing date of your patent application and this product was available earlier than when you first conceived the invention. Next, let's say you decide to enforce your U.S. patent against a competitor, and during the process of litigation, your competitor finds this information.

At a minimum, all the time and expense you put into the effort will have been wasted since your patent could now be invalidated. So remember, full disclosure to your patent professional and to the USPTO is essential! As a side note, if the above scenario is a concern to you or your company, talk to your patent professional about the legal aspects of this scenario as it relates to your concerns.

Of course, the devil is in the details, and you will undoubtedly have many questions during the patent application process. Hey, did you catch that? Questions, you will have many questions about this during the process. So ask your patent professional those questions early! Disclose everything you know to your patent professional and let him or her help you determine what needs to be disclosed to the USPTO.

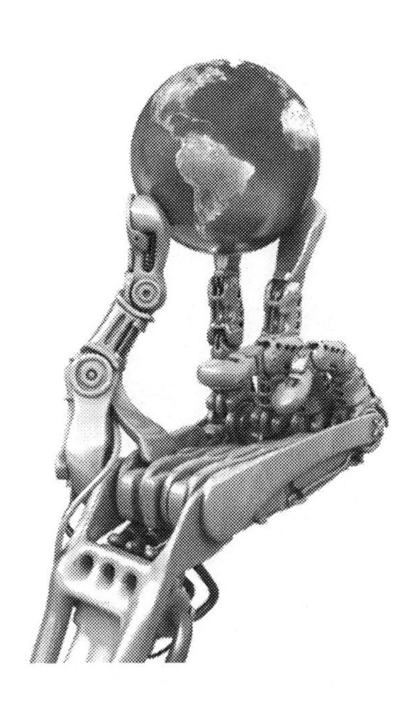

Chapter 9: Changing the World with Ideas for the Future

One comment I hear occasionally is that all inventions being created today are simply add-ons to existing inventions, implying that all we are doing now is simply improving on them. While it is true that we are indeed improving on existing technology and inventions, we are also creating original inventions.

Sure, when we sit back and contemplate a list of all the great inventions of our time, it is impressive and seems like everything we could ever need in our lives has already been invented. But all you have to do is some basic research to verify that such a bold statement is completely false. It is analogous to asking on a road trip, "Are we there yet?" Such a road trip assumes a fixed beginning and a fixed ending, but some journeys do not come to an end.

I believe we are on a never-ending road of discovery. Think of all the new medicines that will be created to target and cure specific illnesses with the discovery of DNA. There is the field of nanotechnologies with the promise to provide new technology by controlling matter on atomic and molecular scale. Green technologies promise a future of technology without fossil fuels. The list is endless.

As such, I know the trip of inventing will never end; there are simply moments in time when big inventions are created. While our inventions have grown exponentially, so too has our technology and our ability to provide new solutions to the growing list of new problems and challenges the world faces. As we learn more, we will discover more, find more problems to solve, develop new technology, and come up with brilliant new inventions. It is a fantastic time to be an inventor, to learn new technologies, and to create new ones.

So to all those who say we are only simply building on inventions or discoveries that have already been made, I say, "Hogwash!" And guess what? The more of us who choose to think like inventors and act on our ideas, the more new inventions there will be!

So with those flawed notions behind us, let's challenge ourselves. Let's use our imagination and solve some of our biggest problems. Sure, many of the new discoveries to come may require technical knowledge or a scientific background, but what if we simply started with a topic that inspired each one of us personally and each of us acted on our little voice?

I am confident that all we need to do is look at the world with no boundaries or limitations, identify those problems we want to solve, and then invent novel solutions. That doesn't mean we all need to work on a perpetual motion machine, but it does mean that we can use the approach presented in this book to invent new products. We can even help the companies we work for develop new products in a challenging marketplace or provide consumers with products that make their lives better.

Ideas for the Future

As each one of us becomes accomplished inventors and innovators, it is our responsibility to also solve problems that make the world a better place. If that sounds a bit corny to you, think again. By putting our brains together, we can create the world's largest human supercomputer of collaborative inventors!

Start with yourself, your company, or how you presently interact with the world, and solve those problems that you encounter with innovation and creativity. Use the skills presented in this book, and your gut, to create solutions. You will be amazed at how fun it will be and how much of an impact you will have.

Imagine how the future will look. How will the technology work? What new technologies will we discover? How will we spend our time? How will we earn a living and raise a family? How will the world's other countries interact with our own and change our lives?

Here are a few of the topics to think about that are in need of invention and innovation:

- Green technologies: What products can we create that use natural renewable resources like solar, wind, magnetic energy, heat, and so on?
- Time: What can we create that would help us get forty-eight hours into a twenty-four-hour day to leave plenty of time to explore hobbies and enjoy family time?
- Charity: How can we take care of the less fortunate and empower them to succeed?
- Education: How can we learn from and build on the lessons of those who lived before us? How can we remember more and recall faster?
- Food: How can we eliminate world hunger and help the needy?
- Consumer products: What new products can we create that help solve a problem or serve an important consumer need?
- New technologies: What new technologies can we build on? What about 3D microprocessors, biological building blocks, nanotechnology, or wireless mesh networks?
- Health care: What can we create for health care? Topics include longevity, cancer cures, and new medicines.

Creatively Inventing Framework Recap

Part I: Four-Step Opportunity Spotlight of the Creatively Inventing Framework was presented in chapter 1 to help you shine a spotlight on the specific problem to be solved and where you will focus.

Part I

1. **Asking questions**
2. **Answering questions**
3. **Refinement**
4. **Problem statement**

In chapter 4, *Part II: Three-Step Inspiration Boost* was presented to help motivate you to get into the proper mind-set for inventing and problem solving.

Part II

1. **Clear the present moment**
2. **Reflect**
3. **Switch to the present moment and think of solutions**

In chapter 5, *Part III: Seven-Step Strategic Planning Process* was presented to support team or group efforts where the ideas identified in the brainstorming session are organized and prioritized into a list used to focus both intellectual property development and product development resources. However, solo inventors may also find Part III useful for their efforts as well.

Note that there is some overlap between steps 1 and 2 in Part III and steps 1 through 4 in Part I. So feel free to use Part I in place of these two steps but make sure to track who came up with the idea. This will be used when associating inventors with the specific ideas generated.

Part III

1. **Brainstorm by asking questions**
2. **Generate answers or solutions (identify who came up with the idea)**
3. **Identify categories for ideas**
4. **Assign a team leader to each category**

5. **Prioritize the categories by value to the company**
6. **Assign each idea to a category**
7. **Prioritize ideas within a category**

A Personal Note

I encourage you to provide me with feedback on your experiences with your invention and innovation journey that you wish to share with the audience of this book.

If I receive enough of these personal experiences, I will compile these inventor journey stories together on the Web site[15] or may even compile them in a follow-up book that can help beginning inventors and motivate even more people to become inventors.

We would love to hear what you invented, why you invented it, your "ah ha" moments, approaches that worked for you, and approaches that didn't.

15 www.thinktekglobally.com.

Epilogue

There are moments through the year where we naturally slow down. Moments such as holidays, family gatherings, reunions, and other moments in time that provide us with slower-paced opportunities where we re-engage our brains, remember our passions, and think. During these moments, we often feel deep emotion from simple things like watching the reunion of a family with their military son, remembering lost loved ones and pets, watching children during the holidays, sharing with family members, and so on.

This was not a book on psychology, but I do know how I feel during these slower moments and how I get inspired when I least expect it. It hits me like a wave of emotion and provides me with motivation to solve a new problem or to solve an existing problem differently. Most of the time, the problem I get motivated to solve is not even related to what triggered my feelings of inspiration. But I get energized and motivated by it.

Why can't we build these slower moments into our daily lives so we feel this inspiration and passion more often? Do we need a reason to slow down and do those things we always wanted to do?

The 2007 movie *The Bucket List* with Jack Nicholson and Morgan Freeman is a good example. In *The Bucket List,* both Nicholson and Freeman have health problems that motivate them to write a list of all the things they want to do before they die (that is, before they kick the bucket). It was a great movie, but it made me wonder if we really need such an intense moment in time to motivate us to make the most of our life?

This subject is a deep one, and oftentimes we avoid thinking about such emotional subjects. But I must admit, I did have one of those moments in my life. I wouldn't say it was a moment in time that caused me to start to dream and think more deeply, as I had been doing that before. But it was a moment in time that impacted me and those around me.

On the week before Thanksgiving in 2004, I was busy hustling and bustling with work-related activities, and my wife was doing the same. One morning, I woke up not feeling too well, and my wife noticed my skin coloring looked very gray. I was having trouble breathing. After a short debate (yes, I tried to convince her I could still go to work for an important meeting), she convinced me to go to the emergency room.

To make a long, painful story short, soon after I arrived in the emergency room, I almost died. I had a pulmonary embolism (also known as PE, or a blood clot in the lung) that made it appear as if I were having heart-related problems. But the emergency room doctors couldn't find a heart problem and were puzzled by my condition.

As I lay in the hallway of the busy emergency room, slowly getting worse, a doctor arrived for her shift, ordered a CT scan, discovered the PE, and saved my life. I spent the next few days in ICU confined to the bed while they ran tests and kept me from moving around, fearing a blood clot would start to move.

Thanks to my wonderful, loving, persistent, and observant wife; a passionate quick-thinking team of doctors; and the hard-working nursing staff at our local hospital, I survived. Needless to say, it was a very intense reminder to me that life is indeed short. I think that was when I actually decided to write a book to communicate how much fun the process of creating, innovating, and patenting can be.

But I am not unique. Many people experience similar moments in their lives where they are forced to slow down. They may have experienced an intense moment personally or have shared one with a family member or close friend. Some people use these opportunities to motivate themselves to create their own personal bucket list, while others go back to their busy lives and put the intensity of the moment behind them.

Why do we really need such intense moments to motivate us and remind us that life is short? Wouldn't it be incredible if we decided to make time in our busy lives to think deeper without having a life-changing moment?

Why not decide that each of us will act on the suggestions I make in this book and be part of a global collaboration of innovators and innovation teams determined to solve problems? From personal problems to business problems to the world's social and environmental problems, each of us can find that place where we make a difference. Become inspired, let the passion motivate you, and most of all, be thankful for the life you have.

Listen to your inner child, empower your creative self, look at the world anew, clear your head, reflect, and become inspired. Build a team of people inspired in similar topics to leverage your collective brainpower and get those creative juices flowing. Put together a team of creative people at your workplace and get them working on challenges together. Collaborate by linking your collective brain processors together into a large human supercomputer. Then find the time to think about how you will make a difference.

We began our journey in this book with the simple concept of taking more time to think deeper and act on your ideas while empowering yourself to look at the world with a childlike curiosity.

This book has presented useful tools and the inspiration to think, create, and become more involved in solving the problems you see. Whether you decide to focus on problems at home, at work, or in academia, or on larger social problems, you can make a difference by simply slowing down, looking around you, following your passions, and taking time to think deeper about what you see. What problems will you solve? How can you make a difference?

Your ideas may not result in a patent application, but if your ideas drive you to apply for a patent, this book has provided you with information that can help you. Regardless of the problems or ideas you decide to focus on, the problem-solving techniques presented in this book will help you achieve your goals.

Applying these techniques will focus your thinking and help you to apply yourself to solve the problems you set your mind to solve. By acting on moments of inspiration and following your passions, you will be amazed at the results and the impact you will have. You can make a difference. Believe it. Never doubt it. Simply *live your dreams, follow your passions, and turn your dreams into reality!*

"May you live in interesting times"; so says the ancient Chinese curse. We are confronted with many large challenges in the world today. But with challenge comes opportunity, as each of us looks for new solutions to those challenges.

Now is the time for you to act on your ideas! Think of positive impacts you can have with your ideas. You are still not sure, you say? Well, just remember, one idea leads to another and to another, and so on. Before you know it, you could be solving problems with solutions you never thought you had.

If you still don't think you can become inspired to solve problems, I say, "Hogwash!" You can and will, but you must first take action. Just by the very fact that you have read this book, I know you are curious about inventing. So what are you waiting for? Get started solving problems today!

And now your personal journey begins as you join our exclusive group of innovative inventors *acting on your ideas using the Creatively Inventing Framework.*

Appendix A: What Is a Patent?

By Pin Tan, published with permission of Weide & Miller, Ltd. in Las Vegas, Nevada

What Is a Patent?

A patent for an invention is the grant of a property right to the inventor, issued by the United States Patent and Trademark Office (USPTO). Generally, the term of a new patent is twenty years from the date on which the application for the patent was filed in the United States or, in special cases, from the date an earlier related application was filed, subject to the payment of maintenance fees. U.S. patent grants are effective only within the United States, U.S. territories, and U.S. possessions. Under certain circumstances, patent term extensions or adjustments may be available.

The right conferred by the patent is the "right to exclude others from making, using, offering for sale, or selling" the invention in the United

States or importing the invention into the United States. What is NOT granted is the right to make, use, offer for sale, sell, or import, ONLY the right to exclude others from making, using, offering for sale, selling, or importing the invention. Once a patent is issued, the patent owner must enforce the patent, thus it is a private cause of action.

There are three types of patents: utility patents, design patents, and plant patents. Utility patents may be granted to anyone who invents or discovers any new and useful process, machine, article of manufacture, or composition of matter, or any new and useful improvement thereof (which covers just about everything). Utility patents are by far the most common type of patent applied for and granted. Utility patents cover the utilitarian functional aspects of an invention. Just about any type of invention can be protected. The biggest exceptions are mathematical formulas, naturally occurring phenomena, and inventions that "violate the laws of nature," such as a perpetual motion machine.

Design patents may be granted to anyone who invents a new, original, and ornamental design for an article of manufacture. The patent laws provide for the granting of design patents to any person who has invented any new and non-obvious ornamental design for an article of manufacture. The design patent protects only the appearance of an article, not its structural or functional features. The process relating to the review and grant of a design patent is generally the same as that for other types of patents. A design patent has a term of fourteen years from grant, and no fees are necessary to maintain a design patent in force. The specification of a design application is short and ordinarily follows a set form. Only one claim is permitted, following a set form that refers to the drawing(s).

Plant patents may be granted to anyone who invents or discovers and asexually reproduces any distinct and new variety of plant.

The Roots of U.S. Patent Law

The patent laws and patent rights are not a Johnny-come-lately type of government action. The Constitution of the United States gives Congress the power to enact laws relating to patents, in Article I, section 8, which reads "Congress shall have power … to promote the progress of science and useful arts, by securing for limited times to authors and inventors the exclusive right to their respective writings and discoveries."

Under this power, Congress has from time to time enacted various laws relating to patents. The first patent law was enacted in 1790. The patent laws underwent a general revision, which was enacted July 19, 1952, and which came into effect January 1, 1953. It is codified in Title 35, United States Code. Additionally, on November 29, 1999, Congress enacted the American Inventors Protection Act of 1999 (AIPA), which further revised the patent laws. See Public Law 106-113, 113 Stat. 1501 (1999).

The patent law specifies the subject matter for which a patent may be obtained and the conditions for patentability. The law established the United States Patent and Trademark Office to administer the law relating to the granting of patents and contains various other provisions relating to patents.

Types of Subject Matter That Can Be Patented

Determining if something is patentable is a two-part process. First, it must be determined if the invention qualifies as the right type of subject matter. Second, a comparison must be made between what was done before (prior art) and the invention, based on legal standards.

1. Protectable Subject Matter

Almost everything qualifies as patentable subject matter. In the language of the statute, any person who "invents or discovers any new and useful process, machine, manufacture, or composition of matter, or any new and useful improvement thereof, may obtain a patent," subject to the conditions and requirements of the law. The word "process" is defined by law as a process, act, or method, and primarily includes industrial or technical processes. The term "machine" used in the statute needs no explanation. The term "manufacture" refers to articles that are made and includes all manufactured articles. The term "composition of matter" relates to chemical compositions and may include mixtures of ingredients as well as new chemical compounds. These classes of subject matter taken together include practically everything that is made by humans and the processes for making the products.

The patent law specifies that the subject matter must be "useful," but almost everything is useful. The term "useful" in this context refers to the condition that the subject matter has a useful purpose and is operable. In other words, an invention that will not operate to perform the intended purpose would not be called useful and would therefore not be granted a patent.

Some exclusions exist based on interpretations of the statute by the courts. It has been held that the laws of nature, physical phenomena, and abstract ideas are not patentable subject matter. A patent cannot be obtained upon a mere idea or suggestion. The patent is granted upon the new machine, manufacture, and so on, as has been said, and not upon the idea or suggestion of the new machine. A complete description of the actual machine or other subject matter for which a patent is sought is required.

2. Legal Standards: Novelty and Non-Obviousness

If the invention qualifies as the proper type of subject matter, then a comparison occurs between the prior art and the invention. In order for an invention to be patentable, it must be new as defined in the patent law, which provides that an invention cannot be patented if:

"(a) the invention was known or used by others in this country, or patented or described in a printed publication in this or a foreign country, before the invention thereof by the applicant for patent," or

"(b) the invention was patented or described in a printed publication in this or a foreign country or in public use or on sale in this country more than one year prior to the application for patent in the United States."

The following may be helpful to understand these sections of the rules. If the invention has been described in a printed publication anywhere in the world, or if it was known or used by others in the United States before the date that the applicant made his or her invention, a patent cannot be obtained. If the invention has been described in a printed publication anywhere, or has been in public use or on sale in the United States more than one year before the date on which an application for patent is filed in this country, a patent cannot be obtained. In this context, it is immaterial when the invention was made, or whether the printed publication or public use was by the inventor or by someone else. If the inventor describes the invention in a printed publication or uses the invention publicly, or places it on sale, he or she must apply for a patent before one year has gone by, otherwise any right to a patent will be lost.

In accordance with these rules, there is a one-year grace period for filing an application after an invention has been made public. This rule differs from most countries throughout the world, which require "absolute novelty," meaning that an application must generally be filed before any public disclosure of the invention. Another exception to this rule is Canada, which applies a limited twelve-month grace period only as to the inventor's own actions.

Even if the subject matter sought to be patented is not exactly shown by the prior art, and involves one or more differences over the most nearly similar thing already known, a patent may still be refused if the differences would be obvious. The subject matter sought to be patented must be sufficiently different from what has been used or described before that it may be said to be non-obvious to a person having ordinary skill in the area of technology related to the invention. For example, the substitution of one color for another, or changes in size, are ordinarily not patentable.

Who May Obtain a Patent

According to U.S. law, only an inventor may apply for a patent, with certain exceptions. If a person who is not the inventor should apply for a patent, the patent, if it were obtained, would be invalid. The person applying in such a case who falsely states that he or she is the inventor would also be subject to criminal penalties. If an inventor refuses to apply for a patent or cannot be found, a joint inventor or, if there is no joint inventor available, a person having a proprietary interest in the invention may apply on behalf of the non-signing inventor.

If two or more persons make an invention jointly, they apply for a patent as joint inventors. A person who makes only a financial contribution is not a joint inventor and cannot be joined in the application as an inventor. It is possible to correct an innocent mistake in erroneously omitting an inventor or in erroneously naming a person as an inventor.

It is noted that under the laws of most other countries, applications are filed in the name of the owner of the right in the invention. Thus, the applicant is often a business or company in those instances.

Appendix B: The Patent Application Process

By Pin Tan and published with permission of Weide & Miller, Ltd. in Las Vegas, Nevada

The Patent Application Process

In a nutshell, the patent application process starts with the preparation of a patent application, which provides a detailed description of the invention, and filing the application with the United States Patent and Trademark Office, which will determine whether the invention meets the standards for patentability. The following describes the process in more detail.

1. Patent Application Drafting Process

This is where a patent application describing the invention is prepared. In general, this begins by gathering information about the invention.

A nonprovisional application for a patent most often includes the following:

1. A written document that comprises a specification (description and claims), and an oath or declaration;
2. One or more drawings illustrating the invention; and
3. Filing, search, and examination fees.

All application papers must be in the English language, or a translation into the English language will be required. All application papers must be legibly written on only one side either by a typewriter or mechanical printer in permanent dark ink or its equivalent in portrait orientation on flexible, strong, smooth, non-shiny, durable, and white paper.

The specification must conclude with a claim or claims particularly pointing out and distinctly claiming the subject matter that the applicant regards as the invention. The portion of the application in which the applicant sets forth the claim or claims is an important part of the application, as it is the claims that define the scope of the protection afforded by the patent. More than one claim may be presented provided they differ from each other. Claims may be presented in independent form (e.g., the claim stands by itself) or in dependent form, referring back to and further limiting another claim or claims in the same application.

An application for patent is not forwarded for examination until all required parts, complying with the rules related thereto, are received. If any application is filed without all the required parts for obtaining a filing date (incomplete or defective), the applicant will be notified of the deficiencies and given a time period to complete the application filing (a surcharge may be required)—at which time a filing date as of the date of such a completed submission will be obtained by the applicant. If the omission is not corrected within a specified time period, the application will be returned or otherwise disposed of (i.e., go abandoned).

The majority of attorney or agent fees are generated during the patent application drafting and filing process. The cost generally depends on the complexity of the application (i.e., how long it takes to prepare) and the filing fee.

2. Filing and Prosecuting a Patent Application in the United States

U.S. patent applications are filed with the United States Patent and Trademark Office. Congress established the USPTO to issue patents on behalf of the government.

The USPTO administers the patent laws as they relate to the granting of patents for inventions and performs other duties relating to patents. It examines applications for patents to determine if the applicants are entitled to patents under the law and grants the patents when they are so entitled; it publishes issued patents (most patent applications filed on or after November 29, 2000, at eighteen months from the earliest claimed priority date or about four months after filing date, if such is later than the eighteen-month calculation), and various publications concerning patents; records assignments of patents; maintains a search room for the use of the public to examine issued patents and records; and supplies copies of records and other papers, and the like. Similar functions are performed with respect to the registration of trademarks. As set forth above, the USPTO has no jurisdiction over questions of infringement and the enforcement of patents.

The head of the USPTO is its director. As head of the office, the director superintends or performs all duties respecting the granting and issuing of patents and the registration of trademarks; exercises general supervision over the entire work of the USPTO; prescribes the rules, subject to the approval of the secretary of commerce, for the conduct of proceedings in the USPTO, and for recognition of attorneys and agents; decides various questions brought before the office by petition as prescribed by the rules; and performs other duties necessary and required for the administration of the USPTO.

The work of examining applications for patents is divided among a number of examining technology centers (TC), each TC having jurisdiction over certain assigned fields of technology. Each TC is headed by group directors and staffed by examiners and support staff. The examiners review applications for patents and determine whether patents can be granted. An appeal can be taken to the Board of Patent Appeals and Interferences from their decisions refusing to grant a patent, and a review by the director of the USPTO may be had on other matters by petition. The examiners also identify applications that claim the same invention and may initiate proceedings, known as interferences, to determine who was the first inventor.

Continuations, Continuation-in-Parts, and Divisional Applications

It is possible to file additional patent applications that claim priority to an earlier patent application. The following sets forth the various types of applications that may claim priority to a pending application to obtain additional or different claim coverage for similar or different inventions:

Request for Continued Examination (RCE) Application: This may be filed when an applicant desires continue prosecution of an application. The same application number and file is maintained. An RCE is most often filed when an application is under final rejection and the application does not yet wish to appeal the examiner's final rejection.

Continuation Application: This may be filed when an applicant desires consideration of different claims or wishes to present further evidence. A different application number and file are created.

Divisional Application: This may be filed, in response to a restriction requirement, to protect claimed subject matter that the office has determined is directed toward a different invention.

Continuation-in-Part Application: This may be filed to add additional, new inventions to an application where the parent application is used as the foundation upon which to base the new invention. Priority is claimed to the already disclosed subject matter.

Formal Papers: Oath or Declaration, Signature

"Formal papers" is a commonly used term to define the papers that must be filed, at some point, with the patent application. For example, an oath or declaration of the applicant (inventor) is required by law for nonprovisional applications.

The inventor must make an oath or declaration stating that he or she believes himself or herself to be the original and first inventor of the subject matter of the application, and he or she must make various other statements required by law and various statements required by the

USPTO rules. The oath or declaration must be signed by the inventor in person, or by the person entitled by law to make application on the inventor's behalf. A full first and last name with middle initial or name, if any, and the citizenship of each inventor are required. The home address and mailing address of each inventor are also required.

The filing fee and declaration or oath need not be submitted at the same time as the filing. It is, however, desirable that all parts of the complete application be deposited in the office together; otherwise, each part must be signed and a letter must accompany each part, accurately and clearly connecting it with the other parts of the application. If an application that has been accorded a filing date does not include the filing fee or the oath/declaration, the applicant will be notified and given a time period to pay the filing fee, file an oath/declaration, and pay a surcharge.

All applications received in the USPTO are numbered in sequential order, and the applicant will be informed of the application number and filing date by a filing receipt. The filing date of an application for patent is the date on which a specification (including at least one claim) and any drawings necessary to understand the subject matter sought to be patented are received in the USPTO or the date on which the last part completing the application is received (in the case of a previously incomplete or defective application).

After Filing Process: Duty of Disclosure and Examination

After filing a patent application, there is a duty of disclosure by the inventor and the inventor's attorney/agent, if any. Under this duty, relevant prior art known by the inventor or attorney/agent must be disclosed by submitting one or more Information Disclosure Statements setting forth the known and relevant prior art. It is noted that this duty does not require the inventor or attorney/agent to conduct a search for relevant prior art.

After filing, there are substantial backlogs. The wait for an initial examination of the application and associated Office Action may range from one to five years, depending on the technology of the application, which examiner receives the application, and the luck of the draw.

When considering the patentability of the invention, the examiner reviews the claims of the patent application. The claims may be thought of as defining a specific request for patent protection of the invention. The claims may be drafted and presented broadly or narrowly. Broader claims offer the potential for broader protection, but typically at a greater risk of rejection.

Once the application has been examined, the applicant is notified in writing of the examiner's decision by an Office Action, which is normally mailed to the attorney or agent of record. The reasons for any adverse action or any objection or requirement are set forth in the Office Action, and information or references are given to aid the applicant in judging the propriety of continuing the prosecution of his or her application.

If the claimed invention is not directed to patentable subject matter, the claims will be rejected. If the examiner finds that the claimed invention lacks novelty or differs only in an obvious manner from what is found in the prior art, the claims may also be rejected. It is not uncommon for some or all of the claims to be rejected on the first Office Action by the examiner; relatively few applications are allowed as filed.

Applicant's Reply

The applicant may reply to the Office Action, and the reply is usually a combination of technical and legal arguments. The applicant must request reconsideration in writing and must distinctly and specifically point out the supposed errors in the examiner's Office Action. The applicant must reply to every ground of objection or rejection in the prior Office Action. The applicant's reply must appear throughout to be a bona fide attempt to advance the case to final action or allowance. The mere allegation that the examiner has erred will not be received as a proper reason for such reconsideration.

The applicant may amend the application in response to the Office Action. For example, the applicant may attempt to more particularly claim his or her invention by amending the claims of the application. The specification, claims, and drawings may be amended and revised to correct inaccuracies of description and definition or unnecessary words, and to provide substantial correspondence between the claims, the description, and the drawing.

All amendments of the drawings or specification, and all additions thereto, must not include new matter beyond the original disclosure. Matter not found in either, involving a departure from or an addition to the original disclosure, cannot be added to the application even if supported by a supplemental oath or declaration, and can be shown or claimed only in a separate application.

In amending the application in reply to a rejection, the applicant must clearly point out why he or she thinks the amended claims are patentable in view of the state of the art disclosed by the prior references cited or the objections made. The applicant must also show how the claims as amended avoid such references or objections. After reply by the applicant, the application will be reconsidered, and the applicant will be notified as to the status of the claims, that is, whether the claims are rejected, or objected to, or whether the claims are allowed, in the same manner as after the first examination. Interviews, via telephone or in person, with examiners may be arranged, but an interview does not remove the necessity of replying to Office Actions within the required time.

Time for Reply and Abandonment

The reply of an applicant to an action by the office must be made within a prescribed time limit. The maximum period for reply is set at six months by the statute (35 U.S.C. 133), which also provides that the director may shorten the time for reply to not less than thirty days. The usual period for reply to an Office Action is three months, after which extensions may be paid for a maximum six-month period. The amount of the fee is dependent upon the length of the extension. Extensions of time are generally not available after an application has been allowed. If no reply is received within the time period, the application is considered as abandoned and no longer pending.

Often, on the second or later consideration, such as a second Office Action, the rejection may be made final. The applicant's reply is then limited to appeal in the case of rejection of any claim, and further amendment is restricted. Petition may be taken to the director in the case of objections or requirements not involved in the rejection of any claim. Reply to a final rejection or action must include cancellation of, or appeal from the rejection of, each claim so rejected and, if any claim stands allowed, compliance with any requirement or objection as to form. In making such final rejection, the examiner repeats or states all grounds of rejection then considered applicable to the claims in the application.

Appeal to the Board of Patent Appeals and Interferences and to the Courts

If the examiner persists in the rejection of any of the claims in an application, or if the rejection has been made final, the applicant may appeal to the Board of Patent Appeals and Interferences in the United States Patent and Trademark Office. The Board of Patent Appeals and Interferences usually consists of three members who hear and decide the appeal. An appeal fee is required and the applicant must file a brief to support his or her position. An oral hearing will be held if requested upon payment of the specified fee.

If the decision of the Board of Patent Appeals and Interferences is still adverse to the applicant, an appeal may be taken to the Court of Appeals for the Federal Circuit or a civil action may be filed against the director in the United States District Court for the District of Columbia. The Court of Appeals for the Federal Circuit will review the record made in the office and may affirm or reverse the office's action. In a civil action, the applicant may present testimony in the court, and the court will make a decision.

Allowance and Issue of a Patent

If, on examination of the application, the patent application is found to be allowable, a Notice of Allowance and Fee(s) Due will be sent to the applicant, or to the applicant's attorney or agent of record. A fee must be paid for the patent to issue. If timely payment of the fee(s) is not made, the application will be regarded as abandoned.

When the required fees are paid, the patent issues as soon as possible after the date of payment, which depending upon the volume of printing on hand is usually two to four months. The patent grant then is delivered or mailed on the day of its grant, or as soon thereafter as possible, to the inventor's attorney or agent, if there is one of record, otherwise directly to the inventor. On the date of the grant, the patent file becomes open to the public for applications not opened earlier by publication of the application.

Note Regarding Provisional Patent Applications

Since June 8, 1995, the patent laws have offered inventors the option of filing a provisional patent application. This was designed to provide a lower cost for filing a patent application to obtain a filing date in the United States. Claims are not required for a provisional application. A provisional application provides the means to establish an early effective filing date in a patent application and permits the term "Patent Pending" to be applied in connection with the invention. Provisional applications may not be filed for design inventions.

The filing date of a provisional application is the date on which a written description of the invention and drawings, if any, are filed with the office. To be complete, a provisional application must also include the filing fee and a cover sheet specifying that the application is a provisional application for patent. The applicant then has up to twelve months to file a nonprovisional application for patent. The claimed subject matter in the later filed nonprovisional application is entitled to the benefit of the filing date of the provisional application if it has support in the provisional application.

Provisional applications are *not* examined on their merits and thus cannot issue as patents. A provisional application will become abandoned by operation of law twelve months from its filing date. A provisional application automatically becomes abandoned when its pendency expires twelve months after the provisional application filing date by operation of law. Applicants must file a nonprovisional application claiming benefit of the earlier provisional application filing date in the patent application before the provisional application pendency period expires in order to preserve any benefit from the provisional-application filing.

Beware that an applicant whose invention is "in use" or "on sale" (see 35 U.S.C. §102(b)) in the United States during the one-year provisional-application pendency period may lose more than the benefit of the provisional application filing date if the one-year provisional-application pendency period expires before a corresponding nonprovisional application is filed. Such an applicant may also lose the right to ever patent the invention (see 35 U.S.C. §102(b)).

Provisional patent applications are often misunderstood and misused. There is no such thing as a provisional patent, only provisional patent applications. Inventors should at the very least understand that a provisional application will not mature into a granted patent without further submissions (e.g., a utility patent application).

As you can now see from the example just presented, taking the Invention Disclosure Form and translating it into a patent application is detailed and tedious work that will be done by your patent professional. Conceiving the idea and reducing it to practice is your job. So the more information you provide on your idea, the more complete your patent application will be.

Appendix C: Additional Considerations

By Pin Tan and published with permission of Weide & Miller, Ltd. in Las Vegas, Nevada

Additional Considerations for Patent Applicants

1. Time Bars

Patent applications must be filed timely (in the United State, this is within one year of first public use, disclosure, or offer for sale).

2. Patentability Search

Patent searching may optionally occur at any time, but usually before filing of the patent application to determine if any prior art exists that may prevent the patenting of an inventor's invention. Prior art searching is not 100 percent accurate and thus may miss relevant art. Under the duty of disclosure, the results of prior art searching must be provided to the office, in an Information Disclosure Statement, if an application is filed.

3. Patent Marking and Patent Pending

After a patent has issued, products or services covered by the patent should be marked "Patent Pending" to discourage infringement and to provide notice to others. The penalty for failure to mark is that the patentee may not recover damages from an infringer unless the infringer was duly notified of the infringement and continued to infringe after the notice.

The marking of an article as patented when it is not in fact patented is against the law and subjects the offender to a penalty. Some persons mark articles sold with the terms "Patent Applied For" or "Patent Pending." These phrases have no legal effect, but only give information that an application for patent has been filed in the USPTO. The protection afforded by a patent does not start until the actual grant of the patent. False use of these phrases or their equivalent is prohibited.

4. Assignments and Licenses

A patent is personal property and may be sold to others or mortgaged, just like any other property. For example, a patent may be bequeathed by a will, and it may pass to the heirs of a deceased patentee. The patent law provides for the transfer or sale of a patent, or of an application for patent, by an instrument in writing. Such an instrument is referred to as an assignment and may transfer the entire interest in the patent. The assignee, when the patent is assigned to him or her, becomes the owner of the patent and has the same rights that the original patentee had.

The statute also provides for the assignment of a part interest, that is, a half interest, a fourth interest, and so on, in a patent. There may also be a grant that conveys the same character of interest as an assignment but only for a particularly specified part of the United States.

An assignment, grant, or conveyance of any patent or application for patent should be acknowledged before a notary public to prevent the signature from being challenged. The certificate of such acknowledgment constitutes prima facie evidence of the execution of the assignment, grant, or conveyance.

Recording of Assignments: The office records assignments, grants, and similar instruments sent to it for recording, and the recording serves as notice. If an assignment, grant, or conveyance of a patent or an interest in a patent (or an application for patent) is not recorded in the office within three months from its date, it is void against a subsequent purchaser for a valuable consideration without notice, unless it is recorded prior to the subsequent purchase.

5. Maintenance Fees

All utility patents that issue from applications filed on and after December 12, 1980, are subject to the payment of maintenance fees, which must be paid to the USPTO to maintain the patent in force. These fees are due between the three- to four-year window, the seven- to eight-year window, and the eleven- to twelve-year window. Payments in the last six months of the window periods require an additional surcharge with the payment. Failure to pay the current maintenance fee on time may result in expiration of the patent.

6. Life of a Patent: Rights Granted and Enforcement

A U.S. patent grant confers "the right to exclude others from making, using, offering for sale, or selling the invention throughout the United States or importing the invention into the United States" and its territories and possessions for the term of the patent.

The exact nature of the right conferred must be carefully distinguished, and the key is in the words "right to exclude" in the phrase just quoted. The patent does not grant the right to make, use, offer for sale, or sell or import the invention but only grants the exclusive nature of the right. Any person is ordinarily free to make, use, offer for sale, or sell or import anything he or she pleases, and a grant from the government is not necessary. The patent only grants the right to exclude others from making, using, offering for sale, or selling or importing the invention.

Since the patent does not grant the right to make, use, offer for sale, or sell, or import the invention, the patentee's own right to do so is dependent upon the rights of others and whatever general laws might be applicable. A patentee, merely because he or she has received a patent for an invention, is not thereby authorized to make, use, offer for sale, or sell, or import the invention if doing so would violate any law. An inventor of a new automobile who has obtained a patent thereon would not be entitled to use the patented automobile in violation of the laws of a state requiring a license, nor may a patentee sell an article, the sale of which may be forbidden by a law, merely because a patent has been obtained.

Neither may a patentee make, use, offer for sale, or sell, or import his or her own invention if doing so would infringe the prior rights of others. It is possible, but fairly uncommon, for a patented invention to also be covered by the patent of another. Ordinarily there is nothing that prohibits a patentee from making, using, offering for sale, or selling, or importing his or her own invention, unless he or she thereby infringes another's patent, which is still in force. For example, a patent for an improvement of an original device already patented would be subject to the patent on the device.

The term of the patent shall be generally twenty years from the date on which the application for the patent was filed in the United States or, if the application contains a specific reference to an earlier filed application under 35 U.S.C. 120, 121, or 365(c), from the date of the earliest such application was filed, and subject to the payment of maintenance fees as provided by law and as set forth above.

7. Foreign Applicants for U.S. Patents

The patent laws of the United States make no discrimination with respect to the citizenship of the inventor. Thus, any inventor, regardless of his or her citizenship, may apply for a patent on the same basis as a U.S. citizen. There are, however, a number of particular points of special interest to applicants located in foreign countries. The application for patent in the United States must be made by the inventor, and the inventor must sign the oath or declaration (with certain exceptions), which differs from the law in many countries, where the signature of the inventor and an oath of inventorship are not necessary.

An application for a patent filed in the United States by any person who has previously regularly filed an application for a patent for the same invention in a foreign country which affords similar privileges to citizens of the United States shall have the same force and effect for the purpose of overcoming intervening acts of others as if filed in the United States on the date on which the application for a patent for the same invention was first filed in such foreign country. This is the case, provided the application in the United States is filed within twelve months (six months in the case of a design patent) from the earliest date on which any such foreign application was filed and claims priority under 35 U.S.C. 119(b) to the foreign application.

If any application for patent has been filed in any foreign country by the applicant or by his or her legal representatives or assigns prior to his or her application in the United States, then priority may be claimed to this foreign application. Claiming priority to the foreign application allows the applicant to "jump ahead" of other prior art. A foreign applicant may be represented by any patent attorney or agent who is registered to practice before the USPTO. Foreign attorneys or agents may not practice in the United States before the USPTO without first being registered by the office.

8. Foreign Patents

Since the rights granted by a United States patent extend only throughout the territory of the United States and have no effect in a foreign country, an inventor who wishes patent protection in other countries must apply for a patent in each of the other countries or in regional patent offices. Almost every country has its own patent law, and a person desiring a patent in a particular country must make an application for patent in that country, in accordance with the requirements of that country.

The laws of many countries differ in various respects from the patent law of the United States, although more recently the laws of the United States have been amended to more closely resemble the foreign rules. In most foreign countries, publication of the invention before the date of the application will bar the right to a patent. In most foreign countries, maintenance fees are required.

There is a treaty relating to patents that is adhered to by 168 countries, including the United States, and is known as the Paris Convention for the Protection of Industrial Property. It provides that each country guarantees to the citizens of the other countries the same rights in patent and trademark matters that it gives to its own citizens. Applications filed under these provisions are most often called PCT-type applications. The treaty also provides for the right of priority in the case of patents, trademarks, and industrial designs (design patents). This right means that, on the basis of a regular first application filed in one of the member countries, the applicant may, within a certain period of time, apply for protection in all the other member countries. These later applications will then be regarded as if they had been filed on the same day as the first application. Thus, these later applicants will have priority over applications for the same invention that may have been filed during the same period of time by other persons. Moreover, these later applications, being based on the first application, will not be invalidated by any acts accomplished in the interval, such as, for example, publication or exploitation of the invention, or the sale of copies of the design. This may referred to as "jumping ahead" of these prior art references. The period of time mentioned above, within which the subsequent applications may be filed in the other countries, is twelve months in the case of first applications for patent and six months in the case of industrial designs and trademarks.

It is also possible to file directly in a particular foreign country, instead of via a PCT-type application. In addition, one need not file in the United States at all, as it is possible to file directly in foreign countries and not in the United States. For all foreign filings, absolute novelty before the earliest priority date is required. Most often, an attorney or agent may be contacted to perform the filing in the foreign country. Costs for foreign filing are dependent on the country, with costs in some countries, particularly European countries and Japan, being on the higher end of the cost scale.

Appendix D: Infringement of Patents

By Pin Tan and published with permission of Weide & Miller, Ltd. in Las Vegas, Nevada

Infringement

Infringement of a patent consists of the unauthorized making, using, offering for sale, or selling any patented invention within the United States or U.S. territories, or importing into the United States any patented invention during the term of the patent. It is noted that in examining applications for patent, no determination is made by the USPTO as to whether the invention sought to be patented infringes any prior patent. An improvement invention may be patentable, but it might infringe a prior unexpired patent for the invention improved upon, if there is one.

If a patent is infringed, the patentee (patent holder) may sue for relief in the appropriate federal court. The patentee may ask the court for an injunction to prevent the continuation of the infringement and may also ask the court for an award of damages because of the infringement.

In such an infringement suit, the defendant may raise the question of the validity of the patent and argue that his or her product is not covered by the claims. For example, the defendant may argue that what is being done does not constitute infringement.

Infringement is determined primarily by the language of the claims of the patent, and if what the defendant is doing or making does not fall within the language of any of the claims of the patent, there is no literal infringement. Even if there is no literal infringement, infringement may be found under the equitable Doctrine of Equivalents, in accordance with which inventions that are substantially the same but slightly avoid the literal language may still be deemed infringing.

Infringement analysis and claim interpretation and application is a complex legal process based on years of court rulings. In general, while the claims are interpreted in view of the specification, they are limited to what is described in the specification. Thus, though a patent may detail a particular configuration of an invention in the drawings and specification, the claims may claim the invention much more broadly.

Suits for infringement of patents follow the rules of procedure of the federal courts. From the decision of the district court, there is an appeal to the Court of Appeals for the Federal Circuit. The Supreme Court may thereafter take a case by writ of certiorari.

Appendix E: Example Invention Disclosure Form Template

1. Title of Invention

2. Inventors

Inventor 1 to n:
For each inventor, list:

- Telephone number
- E-mail
- Address

3. Problem Solved by Invention

4. Previous Solutions or Closest Art

5. Solution

6. Differences/Advantages over the Current State of the Art

7. Disclosures

8. When was the invention was first conceived or realized?

9. Inventor signature(s):

__________________________ Date : _______________
Inventor 1

__________________________ Date : _______________
Inventor *N*

Appendix F: Web Site References

Here are just a few interesting free Web site resources you may find interesting or useful.

www.thinktekglobally.com	Think Tek, Inc.–Think Globally Web site and resource link related to this book
www.uspto.gov	USPTO Web site on patents and trademarks
uspto.gov/patents/basics/index.html	USPTO general information concerning patents
www.google.com/Patents	Free search engine for searching for patents and patent publications
patft.uspto.gov/	USPTO free patent publication search engine
www.uiausa.org/	UIA is dedicated to inventor education and support

oedci.uspto.gov/OEDCI/GeoRegion.jsp	Search for a qualified patent professional (attorney or agent)
www.freePatentsonline.com/	Free search engine for searching patents and patent publications
howstuffworks.com	Useful research Web site
www.ask.com	Useful research Web site
www.wikipedia.org/	Free online encyclopedia
www.cincinnatilibrary.org/resources/research.asp	Collection of databases to locate information on a broad range of subjects from magazines, newspapers, encyclopedias, and books
library.case.edu/databases/	Research databases
www.TED.com	Excellent Web site for informational videos
www.asknature.org/	Nature-inspired designs
www.cipo.ic.gc.ca/eic/site/cipoInternet-Internetopic.nsf/eng/Home	Canadian Patent Office
ep.espacenet.com/	European Patent Office
ipaustralia.gov.au	Australian Patent Office
www.jpo.go.jp	Japan Patent Office